Mridula Baljekar's

R E A L

❖BALTI❖

COOKBOOK

DEDICATION
*In memory of my beloved parents, Dwarka Nath and Kusum Hazarika,
both of whom died when still quite young.*

Acknowledgements

My thanks to Dr. K. T. Achaya, the author of *Indian Food, a Historical Companion*, which has been invaluable in collecting information about the food items, cooking utensils and eating habits of the two early civilisations: the Harappan and the Indus Valley. The book also has a wealth of information about regional Indian cuisine, both modern and ancient.

Kathleen Cox's superb book, Fodor's *The Himalayan Countries* has been a wonderful guide through the North West Frontier Province where Baltistan is situated.

Some of the historical facts have been extracted from *The Reader's Digest Library of Modern Knowledge*.

I thank the following Balti restaurants for their enthusiasm in informing me about Balti food in Britain and how they cope with the varying demands of their customers:

Planet Pappodum, Chelsea, London
Royal Naim, Birmingham
Sher Khan, Birmingham
Adil's Balti House, Birmingham
'I am the King of Balti', Birmingham

Multitude of loving thanks to my husband, Suhas, for his help and support. Last, but not least, I thank my two young daughters, Maneesha and Sneha, for being so understanding during the time of writing this book.

Mridula Baljekar's

REAL

BALTI
COOKBOOK

EBURY PRESS
LONDON

First published in 1996

1 3 5 7 9 10 8 6 4 2

First published in the United Kingdom in 1996 by Ebury Press
Random House, 20 Vauxhall Bridge Road, London SW1V 2SA

Random House Australia (Pty) Limited
20 Alfred Street, Milsons Point, Sydney,
New South Wales 2061, Australia

Random House New Zealand Limited
18 Poland Road, Glenfield,
Auckland 10, New Zealand

Random House South Africa (Pty) Limited
PO Box 337, Bergvlei, South Africa

Random House UK Limited Reg. No. 954009

A CIP catalogue record for this book is available from the British Library.

Edited by **Felicity Jackson**
Designed by **Sara Kidd**
Photography by **Ken Field**

ISBN 0 09 180975 4

Printed and bound in Great Britain by Butler and Tanner Ltd, Frome and London.

CONTENTS

INTRODUCTION

As recently as 1994, hardly anybody in India had heard of 'Balti' cooking. When I visited there in February 1995, I was asked by many 'What is this Balti craze that is spreading throughout Britain?'

I was born in Assam, in the eastern foothills of the Himalayas, and I certainly had never heard this name mentioned. This was quite surprising as I had been taught by both my mother and grandmother, and they had never talked about Balti, even though they had over 100 years of inherited cooking experience between them.

However, I had watched them cook many mouth-watering dishes in the popular North Indian way in a karahi, the traditional circular, two-handled cooking pan. When I visited a restaurant in Birmingham that was serving food cooked in these pans I made the link between Balti and karahi. Now there are hundreds of Balti restaurants, so-called because most of them are owned by Pakistanis, and Baltistan is now part of Pakistan. If Indians had hit upon the idea of promoting this style of food, I am sure it would have been called 'Karahi cooking'.

Creation of Baltistan

Baltistan is one of the remotest parts of the world, sheltered within the triangle formed by the world's highest mountain ranges, the Himalayas, the Hindu Kush and the Karakoram. The average height of the mountains is at least 7,000 metres; some peaks rise to 8,000 metres and more, and the lowest valley is a minimum height of 2,800 metres above sea level.

The first settlers there were nomads. Thousands of years ago, small bands of people carrying most of their belongings—a curious combination of cloth and leather, earth and metal—on their backs, heads bowed against the ferocious wind, leaning on tent-pole walking sticks for balance, made the arduous journey from Tibet.

Setting up camp at the end of the day, they would lay out their belongings and set up a temporary kitchen. A depression was made in the ground. Its base was layered with tinder, bark and wood. A fire was lit and everyone gathered around. Skewers pierced cubes of meat. Flour was added to water and kneaded into a dough to make a naan which, when lifted, formed a tear-drop shape. The cooked naan was deftly picked off and laid in the centre of the diners. Everyone broke off a piece and denuded the skewers of their juicy contents. The meal was completed: no plates, no cutlery and hardly any washing up! Because of the high altitude and intense cold, the Baltis had to perfect an all-in-one technique which made cooking quick, simple and efficient.

As the embers slowly died down, lentils, meat or poultry were mixed with water, herbs and spices and put into a pot to cook slowly, ready for the next meal. Using a touch more herbs and spices, these were then stir-fried, in a heavy cast-iron pan which had two handles, to make a wholesome and tasty meal. When ready, the pan was placed in the centre and the eaters scooped up the curry with a piece of naan.

Little did this band of nomads realise how popular their style of cooking would become! The technique spread south, east and west, and assumed different names: Balti, Kadhai, Karahi and Wok.

Over the years these bands grew into hamlets and villages. In spite of this evolution, they continued to use cooking methods and utensils which had suited them well during their travelling era. They called the region Balti-stan. The word 'stan' means a dais or large pedestal. It is also used to indicate the domain of a particular race of people. Thus you get Hind-stan (India), Paki-stan, Baluchi-stan and Afghani-stan.

When you take a closer look at the land, you soon find the reasons why the Baltis put down their roots there: lush green valleys dotted with huge lakes; meaty animals grazing peacefully; birds of various hues and sizes. But, above all, the mighty river Indus and its tributaries rising high in the glacial peaks and bringing with them tons of silt which is deposited in the valleys, covering them with a topsoil which is fertile beyond belief.

In the 15th century AD, the Muslims, under their Emperor Akbar, invaded India through the Khyber Pass and firmly entrenched Islam as the main belief in this region. It remains so to this day.

When initially the Portuguese, and finally the British, established their Empire in India, they acquired supremacy of the Asian maritime routes. This diminished the importance of the so-called 'Spice Route', which had passed through Baltistan for centuries and had been the main trade route between Asia and Europe. The British regarded the Khyber Pass as a critical 'high ground' to be held at all costs. It was a key location, the securing of which would prevent foreign invaders entering India. What the British were unable to do, however, was to reconcile the Hindu and Muslim factions within India. They had to resort to Partitioning the country into Hindu India and Muslim Pakistan before they left the sub-continent for good in August 1947.

The region of Kashmir proved to be extremely troublesome. It had a Hindu ruler, but the majority of the population was Muslim. The Hindu Rajah hoped that the British would grant him an independent State. He was wrong. The Pathans, from Pakistan, invaded the region from the west in a bloody and savage confrontation. The Government of India counteracted and sent Indian troops to protect the Rajah. A 'Cease Fire Line' (CFL) was drawn across the disputed area by the British but minor altercations take place between India and Pakistan even to this day. The territory above the CFL went to Pakistan. They called it the Federally Administered Northern Areas (FANA). Baltistan ended up in the eastern section of FANA, with Skardu as its capital.

Indian food in Britain

Over forty years ago, the first Indian restaurants gained a foothold in England. A generation of Britons who had fond memories of the 'Raj', found in tandoori everything they were looking for: it had a bright red, adventurous colour but it was not too hot or spicy. It soon became the favourite Indian dish of the 'sahibs'. The shrewd restaurateurs quickly changed the names of their restaurants to include the word 'tandoori'.

Later, as a new young generation travelled more widely, food from European countries was eaten and talked about at most gatherings. People learnt to cook and enjoy food from outside Britain and, in time, focused on variations of Indian dishes. One of the fortunate recipients of this attention was Balti. Though already in existence on restaurant menus under the heading of 'Karahi Gosht' and 'Karahi Chicken', it suddenly came to the forefront with a change of name; and the appetite for Balti swept the country like the 'tandoori' craze of old.

Just as Baltistan is enclosed by the three highest ranges of mountains in the world, the hub of Balti food in Britain is in Birmingham, enclosed in a similar triangle formed by Stratford Road, Ladypool Road and Moseley Road. Here, over a hundred Balti restaurants cater to an ever-increasing demand.

EQUIPMENT
Karahi (Balti pan)
Archaeologists in the Indus Valley sites near Baltistan have discovered remains of copper and cast-iron pots and pans whose shapes and sizes closely resemble utensils used in India today. One example is the karahi or Balti pan, which is a common sight in every domestic and restaurant kitchen and street-side eatery in Northern India and Pakistan.

The authentic pan is made of heavy cast iron with a round bottom and two handles. It looks exactly like a wok. The Balti pans sold in Britain are made of various metals, including stainless steel, in different sizes. They are sturdy and able to withstand the high temperatures required for Balti cooking. Most Asian shops sell these pans; alternatively, you can buy a good, heavy wok from a Chinese supermarket.

Before you use your karahi for the first time you need to season it. First, wash the pan with plenty of hot, soapy water and rinse it well. Dry off all the water by heating the pan over high heat and add about 30 ml (2 tbsp) of any cooking oil. Heat the oil until smoke rises; hold the karahi by its handles and swirl it until the entire inner surface is coated with a thin film of oil. Let the pan cool for a few minutes, pour off the oil and wipe off with absorbent kitchen paper. The pan is now 'seasoned' and ready to use.

Cleaning and storing the pan properly is equally important. Use plenty of hot, soapy water and a non-abrasive cleaning tool. Rinse the pan several times, dry with a cloth, then brush a little oil on the entire inner surface before storing it. This will help to build up a natural non-stick surface on the pan.

Food processor
A food processor will prepare ginger and garlic pastes; chop and slice onions; make chutneys and relishes in no time at all and purée ingredients to perfection. Bread making will seem effortless using a food processor fitted with a dough hook.

Coffee grinder
A coffee grinder is an essential item for efficient Balti cooking. The ancient nomads used a stone base to grind spices; spices were placed on this base and ground with a small cylindrical roller, rather like a rolling pin, using both hands. Now refined and modernised, this method of grinding is still used in most Indian homes. The aroma of freshly ground spices is unmatchable; for this reason alone it is worth investing in a coffee grinder.

ESSENTIAL INGREDIENTS
Ginger and Garlic
Among the fresh ingredients used in Balti and other types of Indian cooking, you will find two recurring

ones: ginger and garlic. Store them both in a cool dry place, away from direct light. As this is also the ideal condition for storing potatoes, I store my ginger and garlic with the potatoes and they keep for 5-6 weeks in perfect condition. The ends of the ginger roots may look slightly dry, but you can easily slice these off and the remainder will be perfect for use.

You can cut down on preparation time if you have ginger and garlic pastes ready to use (see page 12).

Herbs

Fresh coriander is used extensively in Balti cooking. It is more economical to buy a large bunch rather than the small pots and packets of fresh coriander sold in supermarkets. Most good greengrocers and Indian stores sell coriander.

If you plan to use the entire bunch within 4-5 days, put it in a bowl or jug of water. If you want it to keep for 10-12 days store it in the refrigerator. First, remove the roots, then look for any blackened, yellow/brown leaves and remove them. Make sure that there is no moisture present; spread the bunch on some absorbent kitchen paper for an hour or so if you find any moisture in it. When dry, wrap it up in a large piece of foil and put in the refrigerator. Mint is another ingredient which is characteristic of Balti cooking. You can use fresh, dried or preserved mint. To freeze herbs, prepare as above but discard the tough mature stalks. Wash thoroughly, then chop in a food processor or with a sharp knife, Freeze in a plastic bag and break off as much as you need when required for a recipe.

Chillies

Fresh green chillies are used in many Balti recipes. They will keep well in an airtight container in the refrigerator for up to 2 weeks. Wash and dry them thoroughly before storing. Do not remove the stalks as this will allow moisture to get into the chillies and reduce their storage time. Whenever whole chillies are required in a recipe, you can use them with their stalks as this way they look much prettier.

I normally buy a good quantity and wash them thoroughly with the stalks intact. I then freeze them, ready to use any time. They can be chopped or sliced whilst frozen; it is also easier to seed them this way. When a recipe requires whole fresh chillies you can use these straight from the freezer.

STORING AND FREEZING COOKED DISHES

Spicy food is ideal for freezing and the flavours seem enhanced when thawed and reheated. Most spices used in Indian cooking have natural preserving qualities. Added to this is the wide use of tomatoes in Balti cooking. The acid in the tomatoes is a strong natural preservative. Freeze and reheat as follows:

1. Leave the food slightly undercooked,

2. Cool it rapidly. The best way to do this is to tip the food into a large tray (a large roasting tin is ideal) and leave it in a cool place.

3. Once the food has cooled, put it into appropriate containers, label and chill it before putting it in the freezer. It will be perfect for 6-8 months. Unplanned freezing, such as leftovers, should not be kept in the freezer for longer than 2-3 months.

4. Always thaw frozen food thoroughly and slowly. Make sure it is piping hot before you serve it. If you have a temperature probe, check that the reheated food is at least 85°C. You will find a certain amount of water separation once you have thawed a dish, but the dish will return to its normal consistency when reheated, as the water will be absorbed by the meat or vegetables.

To give the food a fresh taste and appearance, heat about 10 ml (2 tsp) vegetable oil in a karahi (Balti pan) over a medium heat. Add a little garam masala (1.25 ml (¼ tsp) or less depending on the quantity of food being reheated) and let it bubble gently for 10-15 seconds. Add the thawed food and increase the heat to high, then stir-fry until heated through, adding a little water if necessary. Add fresh coriander and serve,

GLOSSARY

Anise Seeds (Ajowain or Carum): Anise, which is native to India, looks rather like a celery seed. It is related to caraway and cumin, though in flavour it is more akin to thyme.

Cardamom (Elaichi): Cardamom has been used in Indian cooking since ancient times. Southern India produces an abundance of cardamom, which found its way to Europe via the Spice Route. There are two types of cardamom: the small green ones (Choti Elaichi) and the large, dark brown ones (Badi Elaichi), which are generally referred to as black cardamom. In the West, there is a third variety, white ones obtained by blanching the small green ones. These have a milder flavour.

Cassia and Cinnamon: Cassia, used as cinnamon in Indian cooking, is one of the oldest spices. It is the dried bark of a tropical plant of the same name. Cinnamon is obtained from the dried bark of a plant related to the laurel family. Cinnamon sticks are indigenous to Sri Lanka. Cassia, on the other hand, grows all over the tropical countries. The flavour is similar, but cinnamon is sweeter and more mellow.

Chillies (Mirchi): Two types of chillies are normally used in Indian cooking: fresh green chillies (Hari Mirchi) and dried red chillies (Lal Mirchi). Long slim fresh green chillies are sold in Indian stores. Jalapeno and Serrano chillies from Mexico are more easily available from supermarkets. Although these are not ideal for Indian cooking, they can be used when a recipe calls for fresh green chillies to be chopped or ground. When they are intended to be left whole, the long Indian variety look more attractive.

Coriander seed (Dhaniya): The seeds of the mature coriander plant are a very important ingredient in Indian cooking. The sweet mellow flavour of the seeds blends very well with vegetables.

Cumin (Jeera): Like many spices cumin can be used either whole or ground. A more rounded flavour is obtained if the seeds are roasted and then ground. It is powerfully pungent so only small quantities are used. The whole seeds are used to flavour the oil before the vegetables are cooked in it. There are two varieties, black (kala jeera) and white (safed jeera). Each has its own distinct flavour and one cannot be substituted for the other. Black cumin is sometimes confused with caraway

Curry Leaf (Kari Patta): Grown extensively in the foothills of the Himalayas, these leaves have quite an assertive flavour, and are used to flavour vegetables and pulses. They are sold fresh and dried by Indian grocers. Dried ones can be stored in an airtight jar and the fresh ones, which have a better flavour, can be frozen and used as required.

Dhanna-Jeera Powder: This is a mixture of cumin and coriander seeds which are ground together in a pre-determined quantity of each. The seeds are mixed and ground together, which allows their natural oils to mix at the same time, thus producing a different flavour from using ground coriander and cumin individually. If you cannot get the mix, you can make your own by using 60 per cent coriander seeds and 40 per cent cumin seeds.

Dried Fenugreek (Kasoori Methi): An aromatic herb characteristic of Balti cuisine. It is native to the Mediterranean region and is cultivated in India and Pakistan. Both the seeds and leaves (fresh and dried) are used in cooking, though in Balti cooking the dried leaves are used more commonly.

Fennel (Saunf): These greenish-yellow seeds have a taste similar to anise. They have been used in Indian cooking since ancient times.

Garam Masala: The word 'garam' means heat and 'masala' is blending of spices. The main ingredients are cinnamon or cassia, cardamom, cloves and black pepper. Other spices are added to these, according to preference. Balti garam masala consists mainly of the basic spices with one or two other ingredients.

Ghee (clarified butter): Ghee has a rich flavour and is used liberally in Mogul food .It can be heated to a high temperature without burning. There are two types of ghee, butterfat ghee and vegetable ghee. Butterfat ghee is made from unsalted butter and vegetable ghee from vegetable shortening. Both are available from Indian stores and vegetable ghee is sold by some supermarkets. To make ghee, melt unsalted butter over low heat; it will bubble and splatter as the moisture evaporates. When it stops, continue to heat until the liquid is a clear golden colour and you can see the sediment (milk solids) at the bottom of the pan. This can take 45 minutes. Pour off the butter, leaving the milk solids. Cool slightly, then strain it into a jar through fine muslin. Store at room temperature. Make vegetable ghee the same way using margarine made of vegetable oils.

Onion Seeds (Kalonji): These tiny black seeds are not produced by the onion plant but get their name from their striking resemblance to onion seeds. They used whole for flavouring fish, vegetables, pickles and breads. They are available in all Indian stores.

Paprika: Hungary and Spain produce a mild sweet strain of pepper. Dried and powdered, this is known as paprika. 'Deghi Mirchi', grown in Kashmir is the main plant which is used for making Indian paprika. It is a mild chilli pepper which tints the dishes with a brilliant red colour without making them too hot.

Saffron (Kesar): The crocus grows in Kashmir. Saffron is a highly concentrated ingredient and only minute quantities are required to flavour any dish.

Sesame Seeds (Til): These pale creamy seeds, with a rich and nutty flavour are indigenous to India.

Shahi Jeera (Royal Cumin): A rare variety of cumin, sometimes known as black cumin seeds. It is more expensive than other types, but its delicate and distinctive flavour is well worth the extra expense. The seeds keep well stored in an airtight jar.

Tamarind (Imli): Resembling pea pods when tender, tamarind turns dark brown with a thin hard outer shell when ripe. Chocolate brown flesh is encased in the shell which needs to be seeded before use. The required quantity of the flesh is soaked in hot water, made into a pulp and used in several dishes. These days, ready-to-use concentrated tamarind pulp is sold in Indian stores. Lentils, peas, vegetables and chutneys benefit from its distinctive tangy flavour.

SPICE MIXES, PASTES AND SAUCES

There are some spice mixes and pastes that are used over and over again in Balti cooking, and it is worth preparing a large quantity to have ready to use when required. Although pre-prepared sauces are used in Balti restaurants, they are not often required for homecooking, except for two that I find useful – Kadhai Gravy (Balti Base Sauce) and Makhani Gravy (Butter Sauce). As they freeze well, they can be made in large batches and divided into smaller quantities before freezing. This chapter also includes a recipe for paneer, a versatile Indian cheese used in many different Balti dishes.

Balti Garam Masala

Makes 100 g (4 oz)

Garam masala is made by combining and grinding together selected spices, and the recipe varies from region to region in India. The basic spices are known to create body heat — the word 'garam' means heat and 'masala' is a mixture of spices. Northern garam masala, of which Balti is one variety, is more aromatic than others. Balti garam masala includes warm winter spices such as cardamom, cinnamon, cloves and nutmeg. One or two other ingredients of your choice can be added to these basic spices.

15 g (½ oz) brown cardamom seeds
15 g (½ oz) whole green cardamom pods
25 g (1 oz) cassia bark or cinnamon sticks
15 g (½ oz) cloves

15 g (½ oz) shahi jeera (royal cumin)
7 g (¼ oz) black peppercorns
2 whole nutmegs, lightly crushed

1. Preheat a heavy-based griddle or saucepan over a medium heat and add all the spices. Stir and roast until the spices release their aroma. Do not allow the spices to change colour, they only need warming through to enhance their flavour. Roasting also makes it easier to grind them finely.
2. Remove the pan from heat and transfer the spices to a large plate – if they are left in the hot pan they may overheat. Allow to cool completely, then grind them in batches in a coffee grinder. Mix the ground batches thoroughly.
3. Put the garam masala in a moisture-free, airtight container and use as required. The mixture will remain fresh and full of flavour for 6-8 months.

Tandoori Masala

Makes 75 g (3 oz)

Making your own tandoori masala means it wil be fresh and aromatic. It is the essential oils in whole spices which keep them smelling and tasting fresh, even after they are ground. Prolonged storage will dry out the essential oils and once the oil starts drying, the flavour too starts diminishing. Keep the spice mix in an airtight container and use it within 6 months. Do not be tempted to make too much; it is best to start off with a small quantity. The quantity below will be enough for 6 months even if you cook tandoori dishes two or three times a month. The tandoori colouring used here comes in powder form and is sold by Asian grocers. It is, however, an optional item as it only adds colour and has no flavour of its own.

15 g (½ oz) cumin seeds
15 g (½ oz) white peppercorns
4-6 long, slim dried red chillies, chopped
two 5 cm (2 inch) pieces cassia bark or
    cinnamon stick
seeds from 8 black cardamom pods
8 cloves

5 ml (1 tsp) saffron strands
15 g (½ oz) shahi jeera (royal cumin)
7 g (¼ oz) mace blades or 7.5 ml (1½ tsp)
    ground mace
1 whole nutmeg, crushed
10 ml (2 tsp) tandoori colouring (optional)

1. Mix all the spices together. In a coffee grinder, grind the spices, in several small batches, until they have a fine texture. Mix the ground batches thoroughly and transfer to an airtight container.

Tandoori Chaat Masala

Makes 75 g (3 oz)

This spice mixture is wonderful sprinkled on salads and hot tandoori dishes. There are several brands of chaat masala available in Indian and Pakistani shops, but the one that you make yourself is always much more flavoursome. Black salt, which is excellent for the digestive system, is used in the mixture. This is sold in Indian shops in both ground and whole form. Rock salt is a suitable substitute. Dried mango powder, which is also available from Indian shops, is required for the tangy flavour. Chaat masala will keep well in an airtight container for up to 6 months. It should be used sparingly.

15 g (½ oz) cumin seeds
5 ml (1 tsp) fennel seeds
10 ml (2 tsp) black peppercorns
4-5 long, slim dried red chillies, chopped
15 ml (1 tbsp) dried mint
15 ml (1 tbsp) dried fenugreek leaves (kasoori methi),
    stalks removed

15 g (½ oz) black salt (kala namak) or rock salt
5 g (⅙ oz) dry ginger powder (santh)
15 g (½ oz) mango powder (amchoor)
5 ml (1 tsp) ground asaphoetida (hing)
5 ml (1 tsp) salt

1. Preheat the karahi over a medium heat. When hot, remove from the heat and add the cumin, fennel and black pepper. Stir for 2-3 minutes, until you are able to smell the aroma. Add the chillies, stir them around and leave to cool completely.
2. When cool, put the roasted spices in a coffee grinder and grind until they are half ground. Add the mint and fenugreek leaves in batches and grind until fine. Mix the ground spices with the remaining ingredients and transfer to an airtight container.

Ginger Paste

Makes 225 g (8 oz)

As fresh ginger made into a paste is required for almost every Balti recipe, it is a good idea to keep some ready to use. When buying ginger, make sure you choose young, slim pieces which look moist and feel firm to the touch. Mature ginger has a large amount of fibre which cannot be used.

225 g (8 oz) fresh root ginger

30 ml (2 tbsp) any cooking oil

Using a potato peeler, peel the ginger. Alternatively, it can be scraped with a sharp knife. Chop the ginger roughly and put into a blender with the oil and 45 ml (3 tbsp) water. Process until you have a smooth paste. Transfer it to airtight containers and store in the refrigerator or freeze it. It will remain fresh for up to 2 weeks in the refrigerator. Do not worry if the colour changes a little, this will not affect the flavour.

Garlic Paste

Makes 400 g (14 oz)

8-10 whole heads of garlic, separated into cloves and peeled

30 ml (2 tbsp) any cooking oil

Put the peeled garlic with the oil and 45 ml (3 tbsp) in a blender and process until it is a smooth paste. Transfer the paste to airtight containers and store in the refrigerator or freeze it. It will remain fresh in the refrigerator for up to 2 weeks. The colour may change slightly, but this does not affect the flavour.

Kadhai Gravy

(Balti Base Sauce)
Makes 1.2 litres (2 pints)

A base sauce is essential if restaurants are to cope with their customers' varied requirements. It means they can alter the taste of their dishes quickly by adding different ingredients to the base sauce. Use this sauce for recipes in the Restaurant-style Dishes chapter. For home cooking a base sauce is not essential, but it is handy for quick, mid-week Balti meals.

450 g (1 lb) onions, roughly chopped
40 g (1½ oz) garlic cloves, peeled
40 g (1½ oz) fresh root ginger, peeled and chopped
10 ml (2 tsp) coriander seeds
5 ml (1 tsp) ground turmeric

7.5 ml (1½ tsp) salt
425 g (15 oz) can tomatoes with the juice
15 ml (1 tbsp) paprika
30 ml (2 tbsp) dried fenugreek leaves (kasoori methi)
15 ml (1 tbsp) sunflower or corn oil

1. Put all the ingredients in a large saucepan with 600 ml (1 pint) water. Bring to the boil, reduce the heat to low, cover the pan and simmer for 35-40 minutes.
2. Remove from the heat and allow to cool. When cold, purée in a blender or press through a sieve. Store in the refrigerator. It will keep well for 8-10 days. It can also be divided into smaller quantities and frozen.

Makhani Gravy

(Butter Sauce)
Makes 1.7 litres (3 pints)

Makhani Gravy has a captivating flavour with a silky, rich texture. It is excellent for serving with leftover Tandoori Murgh (see page 68) or Murgh Tikka (see page 69). The gravy can be frozen to use when required, divide it into four portions before freezing and you will have the right quantity for your chosen recipes.

four 5 cm (2 inch) pieces cassia bark or
  cinnamon stick
4 black cardamom pods, the top of each pod
  opened slightly
8 cloves
10 ml (2 tsp) Garlic Paste (see opposite)
10 ml (2 tsp) Ginger Paste (see opposite)
700 g (1½ lb) canned chopped tomatoes including
  the juice

225 g (8 oz) tomato purée
10 ml (2 tsp) salt
10 ml (2 tsp) sugar
5 ml (1 tsp) chilli powder
2-4 whole fresh green chillies
225 g (8 oz) butter
200 ml (7 fl oz) double cream
10 ml (2 tsp) dried fenugreek leaves (kasoori methi),
  stalks removed and pounded

1. Put all the ingredients, except the butter, cream and fenugreek leaves in a saucepan with 600 ml (1 pint) water and bring to the boil. Cover the pan and simmer gently for 30 minutes. Remove the whole spices and chillies. Allow to cool slightly, then purée the mixture in a blender.
2. Return the sauce to the saucepan and place over a medium heat. Add the butter, cream and fenugreek leaves and simmer for 10 minutes.

Paneer

(Indian Cheese)
Makes 225 g (8 oz)

Paneer is an Indian home-made cheese. It is very versatile as well as being an excellent source of protein and calcium, making it ideal for vegetarians. Paneer is available from Asian grocers and larger supermarkets, but it is very easy to make and it does not require any curing or maturing time.

2.7 litres (4 ½ pints) full cream milk

150 ml (¼ pint) lemon juice

1. Heat the milk in a heavy-based saucepan, stirring frequently to prevent it sticking to the bottom of the pan.
2. When the milk begins to rise, add the lemon juice and let it boil until the whey has separated from the curdled milk. This will become obvious after 1-2 minutes when the milk becomes watery and the curds floats to the top.
3. Strain the curdled milk through a piece of fine muslin and tie up the ends loosely, leaving the curds intact. Hang the cloth in a cool place for 1 hour to allow all the liquid to drain off. Alternatively, the cheese can be formed into a block. Hang the muslin for 5-10 minutes only, then roughly shape the cheese, in the cloth, into a block. Place a weight on top and leave for 2-3 hours. Remove it from the muslin and cut into cubes.

MEAT

The climate in the Himalayan region is ideal for rearing lamb, though Baltistanis tend to prefer sheep and goat's meat. On the other side of the border (the Indian part of Kashmir), lamb is more popular. Sheep and goat's meat require prolonged cooking, so Baltistanis take advantage of the dying coal embers in the tandoor (clay oven) to cook meat with a sauce. When cooking has finished for the day, meat is put in a tightly closed pot to cook on the slow burning coals in the tandoor, ready for the next day. The long, gentle cooking imparts a wonderful flavour as the spices are able to penetrate deep inside the meat. To achieve the same effect without a tandoor, you can marinate the meat, then pre-cook it in a saucepan or in the oven. Unlike their traditional Indian counterparts, Balti meat dishes have very little sauce. This dates back to ancient times when a piece of naan was used to scoop up meat, vegetables and lentils from the Balti pan. The thicker and smaller the quantity of sauce, the easier it was to pick up with the bread.

Pre-cooked Lamb for Balti Dishes

As a general rule, about 700 g (1½ lb) of meat is needed for four people, but often this amount will stretch to feed six people if accompanied by vegetables and dhals. When pre-cooking the meat, it is a good idea to cook a large quantity like this and freeze part of it in 700 g (1½ lb) quantities for future use.

2.8 kg (6 lb) boned leg of lamb, cut into 12 mm (½ inch) cubes
125 g (4 oz) natural yogurt
100 ml (4 fl oz) light malt vinegar

5 ml (1 tsp) chilli powder
45 ml (3 tbsp) Ginger Paste (see page 12)
45 ml (3 tbsp) Garlic Paste (see page 12)

1. Mix all ingredients together in a heavy-based saucepan with 750 ml (1¼ pints) water, cover and cook over a medium heat. When the mixture begins to bubble, reduce the heat to low and simmer for 40-45 minutes.
2. Remove the meat with a slotted spoon and strain the stock. Divide the meat into four portions and then divide the stock equally between each portion. It is hard to estimate how much stock you will have as the liquid evaporates at different rates according to the size of the pan used. If the quantity of stock is not enough for a particular recipe, it can be made up with water.
3. Cool the meat and the stock quickly and freeze the surplus meat in containers. Thaw completely before using in your chosen recipe.

Variation: The meat can be cooked in the oven at 190°C (375°F) Mark 5 for 35-40 minutes, if preferred.

Aloo Gosht

(Meat and Potato Curry)
Serves 6

This much-loved dish from the Northern states of India takes me down memory lane. My mother had a special recipe for Aloo Gosht. The air was filled with the aroma of potatoes being fried in hot ghee, and the final 'Tarka' (seasoning), of Northern garam masala and chilli paste, always lured me towards the kitchen! The chilli paste was made from a special variety of chillies which lent the dish a brilliant red colour but did not give it intense heat. For this recipe, however, I have to be content with normal chilli powder!

50 g (2 oz) ghee or 50 ml (2 fl oz) sunflower, corn or vegetable oil
350 g (12 oz) old potatoes, cut into 2.5 cm (1 inch) cubes
5 ml (1 tsp) fennel seeds
6 green cardamom pods, with the tops split to release the flavour
two 5 cm (2 inch) pieces cassia bark or 1 cinnamon stick, halved
1 large onion, finely chopped
10 ml (2 tsp) Garlic Paste (see page 12)
10 ml (2 tsp) Ginger Paste (see page 12)
200 g (7 oz) canned chopped tomatoes with the juice

5 ml (1 tsp) ground fennel
10 ml (2 tsp) ground cumin
5 ml (1 tsp) ground turmeric
5 ml (1 tsp) chilli powder, or to taste
700 g (1½ lb) pre-cooked lamb (see opposite)
450 ml (15 fl oz) meat stock or stock and water
6 ml (1¼ tsp) salt, or to taste
10 ml (2 tsp) ghee
5 ml (1 tsp) Balti Garam Masala (see page 10)
15 ml (1 tbsp) chopped fresh mint or 5 ml (1 tsp) dried mint
15 ml (1 tbsp) chopped fresh coriander

1. Preheat a karahi (Balti pan) over a medium heat for a few seconds, then add the 50 g (2 oz) ghee. When hot and smoke rises, fry the potatoes in batches for 5-6 minutes, until they are browned. If the potatoes stick to the bottom of the karahi, do not worry as long as the crust remains brown and does not blacken. This will add extra flavour to the sauce. Drain on absorbent kitchen paper.

2. Remove the karahi from the heat and allow the ghee to cool slightly, then add the fennel seeds, cardamom and cassia or cinnamon. Place the pan back over a medium heat and stir-fry the spices for 15-20 seconds.

3. Add the onion, garlic and ginger, and stir-fry for 6-7 minutes, or until the onion is just beginning to colour. Add the tomatoes, ground fennel, cumin, turmeric and half the chilli powder, and stir-fry for 4-5 minutes, or until you can see the fat floating on the surface.

4. Add the cooked meat, increase the heat slightly and stir-fry for 3-4 minutes, then add the stock or stock and water, potatoes and salt. Bring to the boil, reduce the heat and simmer, uncovered, for 10-12 minutes, or until the potatoes are tender. Remove from the heat.

5. In a separate karahi, heat the 10 ml (2 tsp) ghee over a medium heat. Mix together the garam masala and remaining chilli powder in a small bowl, and add a little water to make a paste. When the ghee is hot, add the paste and reduce the heat to low. Stir-fry for 1 minute and add 30 ml (2 tbsp) water, then stir the mixture into the cooked meat.

6. Place the karahi containing the meat and potatoes over a medium heat and add the mint and coriander. Stir-fry for 1-2 minutes, then remove from the heat and serve.

Preparation time: 15-20 minutes
Cooking time: 35-40 minutes

Serve with Balti Naan or Pyaz-Pudina ki Roti (see page 108 or 112).

Not suitable for freezing as the potatoes turn mushy when thawed.

Gosht Gulmargi

(Meat Curry Gulmarg Style)
Serves 4

This unusual recipe is named after Gulmarg (Avenue of Flowers), a major tourist town in Kashmir. The breath-taking natural beauty in this extreme northern state is further enhanced by an abundance of exotic fruits and flowers, and the climate suits a wonderful variety of crops, including stone fruits, mustard and the exquisite Basmati rice. Lamb is a very popular meat in Kashmir and mustard oil, which is very pungent, is widely used in the cooking in this region. However, I use sunflower oil which is light and quite easy to cook with. Corn or vegetable oil can be used, if preferred.

150 g (5 oz) thick set natural yogurt
5 ml (1 tsp) Garlic Paste (see page 12)
5 ml (1 tsp) dry ground ginger (santh)
7.5 ml (1½ tsp) ground fennel
15 ml (1 tbsp) ground cumin
25 g (1 oz) besan (gram or chick pea flour), sieved
50 ml (2 fl oz) sunflower, corn or vegetable oil
6 green cardamom pods, the top of each pod split to release the flavour
10-12 black peppercorns

two 5 cm (2 inch) pieces cassia bark or cinnamon stick, halved
1 medium onion, finely sliced
350 ml (12 fl oz) reserved stock or stock and water
700 g (1½ lb) pre-cooked lamb (see page 14)
4 whole fresh green chillies
15 ml (1 tbsp) chopped fresh mint leaves or 5 ml (1 tsp) dried mint
45 ml (3 tbsp) chopped fresh coriander leaves
2.5 ml (½ tsp) Balti Garam Masala (see page 10)

1. Put the yogurt, garlic, dry ginger, fennel, cumin and besan in a mixing bowl and beat with a fork or wire beater until smooth, then set aside.

2. Preheat a karahi (Balti pan) over a medium heat and add the oil. When hot, but not smoking, add the cardamom, black peppercorns and cassia or cinnamon. Stir-fry for 15-20 seconds, then add the onion and stir-fry for 6-7 minutes, or until the onion slices begin to colour.

3. Reduce the heat slightly and gradually pour in the yogurt mixture, stirring at the same time. Still stirring, add the reserved stock or stock and water and bring to simmering point.

4. Add the cooked meat and simmer for 15-20 minutes, until oil begins to float on the surface. Add a little warm water from time to time, if necessary.

5. Add the whole chillies, mint, coriander leaves and garam masala. Increase the heat slightly and stir-fry for 1-2 minutes. Remove from the heat and serve at once.

Preparation time: 10-15 minutes, plus time for pre-cooking the lamb
Cooking time: 30 minutes

Serve with Sada Pulao (see page 104) and Kadhai Sabzi Masala (see page 72).

Not suitable for freezing.

→***Cook's tip:*** Besan has tiny lumps in it, so it must be sieved before use.

Methi Gosht

(Lamb with Fenugreek)
Serves 4

Fenugreek gives this dish a distinctive aromatic flavour. I have used dried fenugreek leaves (kasoori methi), but if you can get fresh fenugreek leaves from an Indian or Pakistani shop use them. You will only need a small bunch.

40 g (1½ oz) ghee or unsalted butter
1 large onion, finely chopped
two 5 cm (2 inch) pieces cassia bark or cinnamon
   stick, halved
10 ml (2 tsp) Ginger Paste (see page 12)
10 ml (2 tsp) Garlic Paste (see page 12)
7.5 ml (1½ tsp) ground cumin
15 ml (1 tbsp) ground coriander
5 ml (1 tsp) ground turmeric
2.5-5 ml (½-1 tsp) chilli powder
225 g (8 oz) canned chopped tomatoes including
   the juice
700 g (1½ lb) pre-cooked lamb (see page 14)

5 ml (1 tsp) salt, or to taste
450 ml (15 fl oz) reserved meat stock
100 ml (4 fl oz) warm water
15 ml (1 tbsp) dried fenugreek leaves (kasoori methi),
   stalks removed and pounded
15 ml (1 tbsp) chopped fresh mint or 5 ml (1 tsp) dried
   mint
2 long thin fresh green chillies
2 fresh red chillies or ¼ sweet red pepper, cut into
   julienne strips
2.5 ml (½ tsp) Balti Garam Masala (see page 10)
45 ml (3 tbsp) chopped fresh coriander leaves

1. Preheat a karahi (Balti pan) over a medium heat for a few seconds and add the ghee or butter. When hot but not smoking, add the onion and cassia or cinnamon and stir-fry for 7-8 minutes, until the onion is soft and lightly browned.

2. Stir in the ginger and garlic, stir-fry for 1 minute, then add the cumin and coriander. Reduce the heat slightly and stir-fry for 1 minute. Add the turmeric and chilli powder and stir-fry for 30 seconds. Add half the tomatoes and stir-fry for 2 minutes, or until the fat surfaces on the spice paste.

3. Add the cooked meat and salt and stir-fry for 2 minutes. Stir in the remaining tomatoes and stir-fry for 3-4 minutes, or until the fat surfaces again.

4. Add the reserved stock, warm water, dried fenugreek leaves and mint, if using. Bring to the boil, reduce the heat to medium and cook for 15-20 minutes, or until the meat is tender and the sauce has thickened.

5. Add the whole green chillies and the red chilli or sweet pepper strips, the fresh mint, garam masala and coriander leaves. Stir-fry for 1-2 minutes, then remove from the heat and serve at once.

Preparation time: 10 minutes
Cooking time: 30 minutes, plus time for pre-cooking the lamb

Serve with Balti Naan (see page 108), accompanied by a dhal or vegetable curry, if wished.

Suitable for freezing.

Rogan Josh

(Rich Red Curry)
Serves 4

Rogan Josh is one of the most popular lamb dishes to have originated in Kashmir. Traditionally, it is cooked in a large amount of ghee (clarified butter) and very little water. At the end of cooking, a rich, red dish is produced with only the ghee visible, no sauce. The rich red colour is achieved by using a type of local flower, not chillies! This version of Rogan Josh is equally delicious.

700 g (1½ lb) boned leg of lamb, cut into 12 mm (½ inch) cubes
75 ml (3 fl oz) natural yogurt
15 ml (1 tbsp) light malt vinegar
15 ml (1 tbsp) Ginger Paste (see page 12)
15 ml (1 tbsp) Garlic Paste (see page 12)
40 g (1½ oz) ghee or unsalted butter
6 green cardamom pods, the top of each pod split to release the flavour
5 ml (1 tsp) shahi jeera (royal cumin)
two 5 cm (2 inch) pieces cassia bark or cinnamon sticks, broken up

1 medium onion, finely chopped
5 ml (1 tsp) ground fennel
15 ml (1 tbsp) ground cumin
2.5 ml (½ tsp) chilli powder, or to taste
350 ml (12 fl oz) warm water
5 ml (1 tsp) salt, or to taste
22.5 ml (1½ tbsp) tomato purée
2.5 ml (½ tsp) Balti Garam Masala (see page 10)
2.5 ml (½ tsp) dried mint
30 ml (2 tbsp) chopped fresh coriander leaves

1. Put the meat into a large mixing bowl and add the yogurt, vinegar, half the ginger and half the garlic. Mix thoroughly, cover the container and leave to marinate in a cool place for 4-6 hours, or overnight, in the refrigerator. Remove from the refrigerator 30 minutes before cooking.
2. Preheat a karahi (Balti pan) over a medium heat for a few seconds and add the ghee or butter. When hot, but not smoking, add the cardamom, shahi jeera and cassia or cinnamon. Stir-fry the spices for 15 seconds, then add the marinated meat. Increase the heat to high and stir-fry for 5 minutes, or until the meat begins to release its juices. Reduce the heat to low, cover the karahi with a lid or a piece of foil and simmer for 20-25 minutes, or until the liquid dries up and the fat is visible.
3. Add the onion, ground fennel, cumin, chilli powder and the remaining ginger and garlic. Reduce the heat to medium and stir-fry for 5 minutes, or until the fat separates from the spices.
4. Stir in the warm water, salt and tomato purée, mix well, then cover the karahi and reduce the heat to low. Simmer for 25-30 minutes, or until the meat is tender.
5. Add the garam masala, mint and fresh coriander and stir-fry for 1-2 minutes. Serve at once.

Preparation time: 25 minutes, plus marinating time
Cooking time: 1 hour 10 minutes

Serve with Balti Naan or Pyaz-Pudina ki Roti (see page 108 or 112), accompanied by Dum Aloo Kashmiri (see page 73).

Suitable for freezing.

Rogan Josh, with Balti Naan

Gosht Khubani

(Lamb with Apricot)
Serves 4

This recipe from the wonderful fruit-laden valley of Kashmir is very light and refreshing, with quite a thin sauce. It is excellent served with basmati rice.

50 g (2 oz) ghee or unsalted butter

2.5 ml (½ tsp) shahi jeera (royal cumin)

6 green cardamom pods, the top of each pod split to release the flavour

2.5 ml (½ tsp) onion seeds (kalonji)

1 large onion, finely sliced

15 ml (1 tbsp) Ginger Paste (see page 12)

10 ml (2 tsp) Garlic Paste (see page 12)

5 ml (1 tsp) chilli powder, or to taste

5 ml (1 tsp) ground turmeric

5 ml (1 tsp) ground cumin

10 ml (2 tsp) ground coriander

700 g (1½ lb) pre-cooked lamb (see page 14)

5 ml (1 tsp) salt, or to taste

350 ml (12 fl oz) reserved stock or stock and water

100 g (4 oz) dried, no-soak ready-to-eat apricots

4 whole cloves

5 cm (2 inch) piece of cassia bark or cinnamon stick, halved

15 g (½ oz) chopped fresh coriander leaves

1. Preheat a karahi (Balti pan) for a few seconds and add the ghee or butter. When hot, but not smoking, add the shahi jeera, cardamom pods and onion seeds and stir-fry for 15-20 seconds.

2. Add the onion slices and stir-fry for 8-10 minutes, until they are lightly browned, reducing the heat for the last 2-3 minutes.

3. Mix in the ginger, garlic, chilli powder, ground turmeric, cumin and coriander and the cooked meat. Stir-fry for 3-4 minutes. As soon as the spices start sticking to the bottom of the pan, add 50 ml (2 fl oz) water, scrape the bottom of the pan and mix the spices with the meat. Stir-fry for a further 1-2 minutes, then repeat the process of adding water, scraping and mixing. Repeat this once more, then add the salt, stock, apricots, cloves and cassia or cinnamon. Bring to the boil, reduce the heat and simmer, uncovered, for 10-12 minutes.

4. Stir in the coriander leaves and serve at once.

Preparation time: 15-20 minutes, plus time for pre-cooking the lamb
Cooking time: 20 minutes

Serve with plain boiled basmati rice.

Suitable for freezing.

Peshawari Gosht

(Lamb Peshawar style)
Serves 4

Peshawari Gosht comes from Peshawar, in the North West Frontier Province (NWFP), a town dominated by the Pathans, the original inhabitants of Afghanistan, but with a rich culinary heritage left by various foreign powers. The NWFP was created by the British to guard India against foreign invasion. It is very close to the Khyber Pass, the natural link between Afghanistan and Pakistan, through which a host of foreign invaders had entered India over the centuries. This dish is light, fresh and aromatic, totally characteristic of Balti cuisine.

50 g (2 oz) ghee or unsalted butter
5 ml (1 tsp) shahi jeera (royal cumin)
6 green cardamom pods, the top of each pod split to release the flavour
two 5 cm (2 inch) pieces cassia bark or cinnamon stick
1 large onion, finely chopped
2.5 ml (½ tsp) teaspoon crushed dried chillies
10 ml (2 tsp) Ginger Paste (see page 12)
10 ml (2 tsp) Garlic Paste (see page 12)
5 ml (1 tsp) ground coriander
10 ml (2 tsp) ground cumin
5 ml (1 tsp) ground turmeric
200 g (7 oz) canned chopped tomatoes with the juice or fresh tomatoes, skinned and chopped

700 g (1½ lb) pre-cooked lamb (see page 14)
15 ml (1 tbsp) tomato purée
5 ml (1 tsp) salt, or to taste
450 ml (15 fl oz) reserved meat stock or stock and water
2.5 ml (½ tsp) teaspoon Balti Garam Masala (see page 10)
1-2 long thin fresh green chillies, seeded and halved lengthways
15 g (½ oz) chopped fresh coriander leaves
15 ml (1 tbsp) chopped fresh mint leaves

1. Preheat a karahi (Balti pan) over a medium heat for a few seconds and add the ghee or butter. When hot, but not smoking, add the shahi jeera, cardamom pods and cassia or cinnamon and stir-fry for 15 seconds.
2. Add the onion and stir-fry for 7-8 minutes, or until the onion is soft and a light golden colour. Add the crushed chillies, ginger, garlic, ground coriander and cumin. Reduce the heat slightly and stir-fry for 1 minute, then add the turmeric and stir-fry for a further 30 seconds, scraping the bottom of the pan and mixing in any spices that stick to the bottom of the karahi.
3. Add the tomatoes and stir-fry for 3-4 minutes, or until fat surfaces on the spice paste. As soon as this happens, add the cooked meat and the tomato purée. Increase the heat to medium and stir-fry for 2 minutes.
4. Stir in the salt and the stock. Increase the heat to high and bring to the boil, then reduce the heat and simmer, uncovered, for 8-10 minutes. Add the garam masala, chillies, coriander leaves and mint. Stir-fry for 1 minute, then serve.

Preparation time: 10-15 minutes
Cooking time: 25 minutes

Serve with Balti Naan (see page 108), plain boiled basmati rice or Tala hua Chawal (see page 103).

Suitable for freezing.

Lahori Dhal Gosht

(Lahore-style Lamb with Lentils)
Serves 4

Named after the city of Lahore, in Northern Pakistan, this hearty meat and lentil dish has a wonderfully aromatic flavour imparted by the warm, winter spices. An added bonus is the nutty flavour of the channa dhal (Bengal gram), available from Indian and Pakistani grocers. If you cannot get channa dhal, use yellow split peas.

175 g (6 oz) channa dhal, picked over, washed and
    soaked overnight
50 g (2 oz) ghee or unsalted butter
two 5 cm (2 inch) pieces cassia bark or cinnamon
    stick, halved
3 black cardamom pods, the top of each pod
    peeled slightly leaving the seeds intact
4 green cardamom pods, the top of each split to
    release the flavour
4 cloves
1 large onion, finely chopped
10 ml (2 tsp) Ginger Paste (see page 12)
10 ml (2 tsp) Garlic Paste (see page 12)
450 g (1 lb) pre-cooked lamb (see page 14)

6.25 ml (1¼ tsp) salt, or to taste
22.5 ml (1½ tbsp) dhanna jeera powder
5 ml (1 tsp) ground turmeric
2.5-5 ml (½-1 tsp) chilli powder
50 g (2 oz) natural yogurt
200 g (7 oz) canned chopped tomatoes with the juice
350 ml (12 fl oz) reserved meat stock
5 ml (1 tsp) dried mint
5 ml (1 tsp) dried fenugreek leaves (kasoori methi),
    stalks removed
4 long slim fresh green chillies
2.5 ml (½ tsp) Balti Garam Masala (see page 10)
45 ml (3 tbsp) chopped fresh coriander leaves

1. Drain the dhal and put in a saucepan with 450 ml (15 fl oz) water. Bring to the boil over a high heat. Reduce the heat to medium and cook, uncovered, for 8-10 minutes, or until the foam subsides. Cover the pan and cook for 15 minutes, or until tender. Remove from the heat and set aside. (The dish can be prepared as far as this a day ahead and stored in the refrigerator.)
2. Preheat a karahi (Balti pan) over a medium heat for a few seconds and add the ghee or butter. When hot, but not smoking, add the cassia or cinnamon, both types of cardamom and the cloves. Stir-fry for 15-20 seconds, then add the onion, ginger and garlic and sir-fry for 7-8 minutes, until the onion is soft and just beginning to brown.
3. Add the meat, salt, dhanna jeera, turmeric and chilli powder and stir-fry for 1 minute. Add the yogurt and stir-fry for a further 1 minute, scraping and mixing in any spices that stick to the karahi.
4. Add the tomatoes and increase the heat slightly. Stir-fry for 5-6 minutes, or until oil is visible again, then add the stock, the cooked dhal and any remaining liquid, mint and fenugreek leaves. Bring to the boil and reduce the heat to medium. Cook, uncovered, for 10 minutes, stirring frequently to ensure that it does not stick to the bottom of the pan.
5. Add the fresh chillies, garam masala and coriander leaves. Cook for 1 minute, then serve.

Preparation time: 20-25 minutes, plus soaking time and time for pre-cooking the lamb
Cooking time: 50 minutes

Serve with Balti Naan or Pyaz-Pudina ki Roti (see page 108 or 112). Any raita or dip can be served with it.

Suitable for freezing.

Lahori Dhal Gosht, with Pyaz-Pudina ki Roti and Gobi Raita

Kadhai Gosht Do-Piaza

(Balti Lamb Do-Piaza)
Serves 4

This recipe is typical of the type of dishes ancient nomads would have prepared, using the dying coal embers of the tandoor to cook the meat overnight before spicing it up in their karahi or Balti pan the following day.

60 ml (4 tbsp) sunflower, corn or vegetable oil
5 ml (1 tsp) fennel seeds
2.5 ml (½ tsp) ground cardamom
2.5 ml (½ tsp) ground cinnamon
7.5 ml (1½ tsp) Ginger Paste (see page 12)
7.5 ml (1½ tsp) Garlic Paste (see page 12)
2 medium onions, finely sliced
5 ml (1 tsp) ground fennel
15 ml (1 tbsp) ground cumin
1.25-2.5 ml (¼-½ tsp) chilli powder
5 ml (1 tsp) paprika
700 g (1½ lb) pre-cooked lamb (see page 14)

5 ml (1 tsp) salt, or to taste
22.5 ml (1½ tbsp) tomato purée
350 ml (12 fl oz) reserved stock or a mixture of
    stock and water
50 g (2 oz) green pepper, cored, seeded and
    diced
50 g (2 oz) red pepper, cored, seeded and diced
2.5 ml (½ tsp) Balti Garam Masala (see page 10)
15 ml (1 tbsp) chopped fresh mint leaves or
    2.5 ml (½ tsp) dried mint
15 g (½ oz) chopped fresh coriander leaves

1. Preheat a karahi (Balti pan) over a medium heat and add the oil. When hot, but not smoking, add the fennel seeds, ground cardamom and cinnamon, quickly followed by the ginger and garlic. Stir-fry for 30 seconds. Add the onions and stir-fry for 7-8 minutes, until they are soft and just beginning to colour.
2. Sprinkle with the ground fennel, cumin, chilli powder and paprika. Stir-fry for 30 seconds.
3. Add the cooked meat and salt and stir-fry for 2-3 minutes, scraping and mixing any spices that stick to the bottom of the karahi.
4. Mix in the tomato purée and stir-fry for 1 minute, then add the stock or stock and water. Bring to the boil, reduce the heat and simmer for 10-12 minutes, uncovered. Add the diced peppers, garam masala, mint and coriander and stir-fry for 2-3 minutes. Serve at once.

Preparation time: 10-15 minutes, plus time for pre-cooking the lamb
Cooking time: 25 minutes

Serve with Balti Naan (see page 108). Baigan Bharta or Kadhai Paneer-Choley
(see page 76 or 81) is an excellent accompaniment.

Suitable for freezing.

Hirran ka Gosht Masala

(Spicy Venison)
Serves 4

Venison brings back fond and exciting childhood memories for me. My grandfather's favourite sport was hunting. Whenever he and one of my uncles, set off on their hunting trips, we used to wait with excitement to see what they would bring back! When they brought back young deer, my mother, accompanied by the family cook, conjured up mouth-watering dishes. This is one of those wonderful dishes we all enjoyed. The full-flavoured meat is excellent with spices.

700 g (1½ lb) venison leg steaks, cut into 12 mm
  (½ inch) cubes
75 g (3 oz) thick set natural yogurt
30 ml (2 tbsp) light malt vinegar
2.5 ml (½ tsp) ground turmeric
5 ml (1 tsp) crushed dried chillies
17.5 ml (3½ tsp) Ginger Paste (see page 12)
17.5 ml (3½ tsp) Garlic Paste (see page 12)
60 ml (4 tbsp) sunflower, corn or vegetable oil
5 ml (1 tsp) fennel seeds
2.5 ml (½ tsp) onion seeds (kalonji)

5 ml (1 tsp) salt, or to taste
1 large onion, finely chopped
10 ml (2 tsp) ground cumin
5 ml (1 tsp) ground coriander
5 ml (1 tsp) ground fennel
2.5 ml (½ tsp) ground turmeric
5 ml (1 tsp) paprika
2.5 ml (½ tsp) chilli powder, or to taste
15 ml (1 tbsp) tomato purée
2.5 ml (½ tsp) Balti Garam Masala (see page 10)
45 ml (3 tbsp) chopped fresh coriander leaves

1. Put the meat cubes in a large bowl and add the yogurt, vinegar, turmeric, crushed chillies and 7.5 ml (1½ tsp) each of the ginger and garlic pastes. Stir to distribute and mix well, then cover and leave to marinate for 4-6 hours, or overnight, in the refrigerator. Bring to room temperature before cooking.
2. Transfer the meat to a saucepan, add 150 ml (¼ pint) water and bring to simmering point. Cover and cook gently for 45-50 minutes. Remove the meat with a slotted spoon. Strain the stock and make up to 450 ml (15 fl oz) with water and set aside.
3. Preheat a karahi (Balti pan) over a medium heat and add the oil. When hot, but not smoking, add the fennel and onion seeds and stir-fry for 15-20 seconds. Add the cooked meat and salt and stir-fry for 4-5 minutes, reducing the heat slightly towards the end.
4. Add all the remaining ginger and garlic and the rest of the ingredients, except the reserved stock, tomato purée, garam masala and coriander leaves. Stir-fry for 3-4 minutes, then add 50 ml (2 fl oz) water and stir-fry for 2-3 minutes. Add the stock and tomato purée. Bring to the boil, reduce the heat and simmer, uncovered, for 10 minutes. Add the garam masala and coriander leaves and simmer for 30 seconds. Serve at once.

Preparation time: 20-25 minutes, plus marinating time
Cooking time: 1¼ hours

Serve with Tala hua Chawal (see page 103) and Kadhai Sabzi Masala (see page 72)

Suitable for freezing.

Overleaf: Kadhai Gosht Do-Piaza (left) and Peshawari Gosht (right) with Balti Naan

Rista

(Meatballs with Cream and Cashew Nuts)
Serves 4

This wonderfully aromatic recipe comes from Kashmir, a region as rich in its culinary heritage as its natural beauty with the snow capped peaks of the Himalayas, the gleaming lakes and abundance of exotic flowers and fruits.

450 g (1 lb) lean minced lamb
15 ml (1 tbsp) natural yogurt
1 egg, beaten
2.5 ml (½ tsp) ground cardamom
2.5 ml (½ tsp) ground nutmeg
2.5 ml (½ tsp) ground cinnamon
2.5 ml (½ tsp) freshly ground black pepper
salt
two 5 cm (2 inch) pieces cassia bark or cinnamon stick
4 green cardamom pods, the top of each pod split, to release the flavour
2 black cardamom pods, the top of each pod split
6 whole cloves

5 ml (1 tsp) ground fennel
5 ml (1 tsp) ground dry ginger (santh)
45 ml (3 tbsp) sunflower, corn or vegetable oil
5 ml (1 tsp) fennel seeds
15 ml (1 tbsp) Garlic Paste (see page 12)
175 g (6 oz) onions, finely chopped
15 ml (1 tbsp) tomato purée
2.5 ml (½ tsp) chilli powder
150 ml (¼ pint) single cream
25 g (1 oz) cashew nuts, coarsely chopped
2.5 ml (½ tsp) Balti Garam Masala (see page 10)
30 ml (2 tbsp) chopped fresh coriander leaves

1. Put the minced lamb in a large mixing bowl and add the yogurt, egg, cardamom, nutmeg, cinnamon, pepper and 2.5 ml (½ tsp) salt. Mash the ingredients with a potato masher until fine. (Alternatively, mix the ingredients in a food processor until the mince is fine.) Divide the mixture into quarters and make five balls (koftas) from each quarter. Put each kofta between your palms and compress it so that it is firm, then rotate between the palms to make it neat and smooth.
2. Bring 300 ml (½ pint) water to the boil in a karahi (Balti pan) or saucepan and add the whole spices, ground fennel and ginger. Arrange the meatballs in the spiced liquid, preferably in a single layer, and bring to the boil. Reduce the heat to medium, cover the karahi with a lid or a piece of foil and cook the meatballs for 15 minutes. Remove from the heat and transfer the meatballs to another dish using a slotted spoon. Strain the stock and set aside.
3. Preheat the karahi over a medium heat for a few seconds and add the oil. When hot, but not smoking, add the fennel seeds and stir-fry for 15 seconds. Add the garlic and stir-fry until it begins to brown, then add the onions. Continue to stir-fry for 5-6 minutes, until the onions are soft and just beginning to brown.
4. Add the tomato purée, chilli powder and 2.5 ml (½ tsp) salt and stir-fry for 15-20 seconds. Add the strained stock, cream, cashew nuts and meatballs. Stir and mix gently, reduce the heat to low, cover the karahi with a lid or a piece of foil and simmer for 15 minutes.
5. Sprinkle with the garam masala and stir in the coriander leaves. Serve at once.

Preparation time: 20-25 minutes
Cooking time: 35-40 minutes

Serve with Mewa Pulao or Sheermal (see page 106 or 110) and any raita.

Suitable for freezing.

Kheema Do-Piaza

(Minced Lamb with two types of onions)
Serves 4

There are two schools of thought about the meaning of the word 'Do-Piaza'. Generally it is believed to mean any meat or poultry dish cooked with twice the normal amount of onions or two different types of onions. Connoisseurs of Mughal cuisine, however, believe that it means any meat or poultry cooked with a vegetable. Whatever the meaning, this dish is made with minced lamb, onion and shallots.

45 ml (3 tbsp) sunflower, corn or vegetable oil
5 ml (1 tsp) cumin seeds
3-4 small whole dried red chillies
10-12 curry leaves
1 medium onion, finely chopped
10 ml (2 tsp) Garlic Paste (see page 12)
15 ml (1 tbsp) Ginger Paste (see page 12)
10 ml (2 tsp) ground coriander
7.5 ml (1½ tsp) ground cumin
450 g (1 lb) lean minced lamb
5 ml (1 tsp) ground turmeric

2.5-5 ml (½-1 tsp) chilli powder
5 ml (1 tsp) salt, or to taste
50 g (2 oz) thick set natural yogurt
200 g (7 oz) shallots
225 g (8 oz) canned chopped tomatoes with the juice
100 ml (4 fl oz) warm water
10 ml (2 tsp) dried fenugreek leaves (kasoori methi), stalks removed
5 ml (1 tsp) dried mint
5 ml (1 tsp) Balti Garam Masala (see page 10)
45 ml (3 tbsp) chopped fresh coriander leaves

1. Preheat a karahi (Balti pan) over a medium heat for a few seconds and add the oil. When hot, but not smoking, add the cumin seeds and immediately follow with the chillies and curry leaves. Allow the chillies to blacken as this will add extra flavour.
2. Add the onion and stir-fry for 6-8 minutes, until it begins to colour. Add the garlic and ginger and stir-fry for 1 minute.
3. Sprinkle in the ground coriander and cumin and stir-fry for 30 seconds. Stir in the mince, increase the heat slightly and stir-fry the mince for 8-10 minutes, or until just beginning to brown.
4. Add the turmeric and chilli powder and stir-fry for 30 seconds. Add the salt, yogurt and whole shallots and stir-fry for 2 minutes. Add the tomatoes and water, bring to the boil, cover the karahi with a lid or a piece of foil and simmer for 25-30 minutes.
5. Add the fenugreek leaves, mint and garam masala and stir-fry for 2 minutes. Stir in the coriander leaves. Serve at once.

Preparation time: 10 minutes
Cooking time: 55 minutes

Serve with Balti Naan (see page 108), accompanied by Amritsari Dhal (see page 86) and a relish of your choice.

Suitable for freezing.

Dahi ka Kheema

(Mince with Yogurt)
Serves 4

For this delectable dish minced lamb is stir-fried with onions and spices, then cooked gently with natural yogurt. I like to serve it garnished with fresh red and green chillies cut into julienne strips. The easiest way to chop or slice chillies, dried or fresh, is with a pair of kitchen scissors. Slit the chillies lengthways first and wash them to remove the seeds. You do not have to eat them unless you feel adventurous! If you don't want to use chillies, garnish with red and green peppers instead.

45 ml (3 tbsp) sunflower, corn or vegetable oil
5 ml (1 tsp) shahi jeera (royal cumin)
two 5 cm (2 inch) pieces cassia bark or cinnamon
  stick, halved
1 large onion, finely chopped
15 ml (1 tbsp) Ginger Paste (see page 12)
15 ml (1 tbsp) Garlic Paste (see page 12)
700 g (1½ lb) lean minced lamb
22.5 ml (1½ tbsp) ground cumin
5 ml (1 tsp) ground turmeric
5 ml (1 tsp) salt, or to taste

5 ml (1 tsp) paprika
200 g (7 oz) thick set natural yogurt, beaten until
  smooth
5 ml (1 tsp) dried mint
200 ml (7 fl oz) warm water
5 ml (1 tsp) Balti Garam Masala (see page 10)
45 ml (3 tbsp) chopped fresh coriander leaves
2 fresh green chillies, seeded and cut into julienne
  strips
2 fresh red chillies, seeded and cut into julienne strips

1. Preheat a karahi (Balti pan) over a medium heat for a few seconds and add the oil. When hot, but not smoking, add the shahi jeera and cassia or cinnamon and stir-fry for 15 seconds. Add the onion and stir-fry for 7-8 minutes, until the onion is soft and just beginning to brown.

2. Stir in the ginger and garlic and stir-fry for 30 seconds. Add the mince and stir-fry for 6-7 minutes, or until the mince is dry.

3. Add the cumin, turmeric, salt and paprika. Stir-fry for 2-3 minutes, then add the yogurt and mint. Stir-fry for 1 minute, then add the warm water. Bring to the boil, cover with a lid or a piece of foil and simmer for 20-25 minutes.

4. Sprinkle in the garam masala and stir-fry for 1 minute. Stir in the coriander leaves. Transfer the kheema to a serving dish, garnish with the chillies and serve at once.

Preparation time: 10 minutes
Cooking time: 40-45 minutes

Serve with Balti Naan or Sheermal (see page 108 or 110). Lobia Khumb or Kadhai Paneer-Choley (see page 84 or 81) makes an excellent accompaniment.

Suitable for freezing.

Dahi ka Kheema with Sheermal

POULTRY

The ancient Baltistanis cooked whole birds by digging a small depression in the ground and lining it with burning embers. The bird was placed on top and covered by more embers. This method has now been refined to a great extent and the ever-popular 'tandoori' owes its origin to this humble, ancient, nomadic cooking style. Chicken, though the most expensive, is also the most popular bird in Baltistan and, indeed, the entire NWFP, but game birds are also excellent cooked Balti style. As with traditional Indian cooking, poultry should always be skinned first. The skin does not allow the flavours to permeate into the meat and the sauce becomes too fatty. In this chapter includes a selection of familiar recipes which I have adapted for Balti cooking plus recipes typical of this region.

Makhani Murgh

(Chicken in a Butter Sauce)
Serves 4

This recipe is a classic example of the ingenious way in which Indian chefs create delicious and exotic dishes from leftover meat and poultry. Here, leftover Tandoori Murgh is gently simmered in a butter and cream sauce.

1 kg (2.2lb) cooked Tandoori Murgh (see page 68)
15 ml (1 tbsp) corn or vegetable oil
5 ml (1 tsp) Garlic Paste (see page 12)
5 ml (1 tsp) Ginger Paste (see page 12)
5 ml (1 tsp) ground cumin
5 ml (1 tsp) ground coriander

2.5 ml (½ tsp) chilli powder, or to taste
750 ml (1¼ pints) Makhani Gravy (see page 13)
2.5 ml (½ tsp) salt, or to taste
30 ml (2 tbsp) chopped fresh coriander leaves
2.5 ml (½ tsp) Balti Garam Masala (see page 10)

1. Remove the bones from the chicken and cut the chicken into 5 cm (2 inch) strips. When the bones are removed you should have about 700 g (1½ lb) chicken.
2. Preheat a karahi (Balti pan) for a few seconds over a medium heat and add the oil. When hot, but not smoking, add the garlic and ginger and stir-fry for 30 seconds, or until they brown slightly.
3. Add the ground cumin and coriander and the chilli powder. Stir-fry for 15-20 seconds, then add the gravy, salt and chicken. Simmer gently, uncovered, until the chicken is heated through.
4. Stir in the coriander leaves and garam masala and serve at once.

Preparation time: 15-20 minutes, plus cooking time for the chicken and Makhani Gravy.
Cooking time: 8-10 minutes

Serve with Balti Naan or Sheermal (see page 108 or 110) and Gobi Raita (see page 117).

Murgh Hara Masala

(Chicken with Green Spices)
Serves 4

A green Indian dish may seem strange as no Indian restaurant serves it; most restaurants seem to have red or brown curries. Indian dishes basically have four main colours: red, brown, green and white. The first three also have varying degrees of colour tones, depending on the ingredients used. Try this delicious chicken dish with its prominent fresh coriander flavour, and I am sure it will become one of your favourites! The chicken is cooked in the traditional style, on the bone. If using Mexican chillies rather than the long, slim Indian ones, reduce the quantity by half. The easiest way to remove the seeds is to slit the chilli lengthways and gently scrape off the seeds with a knife under running water. Washing them after cutting also reduces the pungency of chillies.

700 g (1½ lb) chicken thighs, skinned
3-4 fresh green chillies, seeded and chopped
25 g (1 oz) chopped fresh coriander leaves
30 ml (2 tbsp) chopped fresh mint leaves or 7.5 ml (1½ tsp) dried mint
15 ml (1 tbsp) Ginger Paste (see page 12)
10 ml (2 tsp) Garlic Paste (see page 12)
2.5 ml (½ tsp) ground turmeric
4 green cardamom pods, the top of each pod split to release the flavour
4 cloves

5 cm (2 inch) piece cassia bark or cinnamon stick, halved
15 ml (1 tbsp) dhanna-jeera powder
125 g (4 oz) whole milk natural yogurt, beaten
5 ml (1 tsp) salt, or to taste
1 medium onion, finely sliced
25 g (1 oz) ghee or unsalted butter
1 small red pepper, cored, seeded and cut into julienne strips
2.5 ml (½ tsp) Balti Garam Masala (see page 10)
15 ml (1 tbsp) lime juice

1. Put the chicken in a karahi (Balti pan) and add all the ingredients except the onion, ghee or butter, pepper, garam masala and lime juice. Place the karahi over a medium heat and stir until the contents begin to sizzle. Reduce the heat to low, cover the karahi and cook for 35-40 minutes, or until the chicken is tender.
2. Increase the heat to medium and add the sliced onion. Continue to cook, uncovered, until all the liquid evaporates, stirring frequently.
3. Add the ghee or butter, reduce the heat to low and stir-fry the chicken for 4-5 minutes.
4. Add the peppers and garam masala, stir-fry for 2-3 minutes, then add the lime juice. Stir well to mix all the ingredients before serving.

Preparation time: 15 minutes
Cooking time: 40-45 minutes

Serve with Balti Naan or Tala hua Chawal (see page 108 or 103), and Aloo-Brinjal or Lobia Khumb (see page 74 or 84)

Suitable for freezing. For best results, freeze at the end of step 1. Thaw completely before proceeding from step 2. At the end of step 1, you can also store it in the refrigerator for up to 48 hours.

Overleaf: Murgh Hara Masala (left) and Makhani Murgh (right) with Tala hua Chawal

Do-Piaza Murgh

(Chicken Do-Piaza)
Serves 4

'Do-Piaza' is a Mogul term, the meaning of which remains controversial. Popularly, it is taken to mean a 'meat or poultry dish with twice the normal amount of onions'. The word 'Do' means twice and 'Piaza' implies 'with onions'. But connoisseurs say that the correct meaning is 'any meat or poultry cooked with vegetables'. Here, I offer you my creation with two different types of onions.

700 g (1½ lb) boned chicken thighs or breast, skinned and cut into 5 cm (2 inch) cubes
15 ml (1 tbsp) lemon juice
5 ml (1 tsp) salt, or to taste
1 large onion, roughly chopped
2-3 long, slim dried red chillies, roughly chopped
60 ml (4 tbsp) sunflower, corn or vegetable oil
2 red onions, finely sliced
15 ml (1 tbsp) Ginger Paste (see page 12)
15 ml (1 tbsp) Garlic Paste (see page 12)
15 ml (1 tbsp) dhanna-jeera powder
5 ml (1 tsp) ground turmeric
225 g (8 oz) fresh tomatoes, skinned and chopped or canned chopped tomatoes with the juice

15 ml (1 tbsp) tomato purée
two 5 cm (2 inch) pieces cassia bark or cinnamon sticks, halved
2 black cardamom pods, the top of each pod split to release the flavour
4 cloves
225 ml (8 fl oz) warm water
15 ml (1 tbsp) chopped fresh mint leaves or 5 ml (1 tsp) dried mint
4-5 whole fresh green chillies
45 ml (3 tbsp) chopped fresh coriander leaves

1. Put the chicken in a mixing bowl and add the lemon juice and salt. Mix thoroughly, cover the bowl and set aside for 15-20 minutes. Meanwhile, put the chopped onion and red chillies in a blender or food processor with 30-45 ml (2-3 tbsp) water and blend to a purée.

2. Preheat a karahi (Balti pan) over a medium heat for a few seconds and add the oil. When hot, stir-fry the red onions for 5-6 minutes, until they soften. Add the puréed ingredients, ginger and garlic and stir-fry for 4-5 minutes, making sure that any spices that stick to the bottom and sides of the pan are scraped and stirred into the onions. One of the characteristic flavours of Balti cooking comes from this action. Make sure the spices that stick to the pan are not allowed to burn by continuously scraping and stirring them.

3. Add the dhanna-jeera powder and turmeric and stir-fry for 30 seconds. Add the tomatoes, stir-fry for 2-3 minutes, then add the chicken. Increase the heat to high and stir-fry the chicken for 4-5 minutes, or until it loses its pink colour.

4. Add the tomato purée, cassia or cinnamon, cardamom and cloves. Stir-fry for 30 seconds and add the warm water. Bring to the boil, reduce the heat to low and cover the karahi with a lid or piece of foil. Cook for 15-20 minutes, stirring occasionally.

5. Remove the lid and increase the heat to medium. Add the mint, fresh chillies and coriander leaves. Stir-fry for 1-2 minutes, then serve.

Preparation time: 20 minutes
Cooking time: 30 minutes

Serve with Balti Naan (see page 108) and Baigan Bharta (see page 76) or Pudina-Dhaniya ki Chutney (see page 114)

Suitable for freezing.

Turkey Narangi

(Turkey with Orange Juice)
Serves 4

A refreshing dish, ideal for the summer months, though equally enjoyable in the winter. As well as using raw turkey meat, you can use leftover Christmas turkey cut into neat pieces. If you use cooked turkey, allow the meat to rest for a couple of hours before using. This helps the pre-cooked meat to absorb the flavours fully.

50 g (2 oz) ghee or unsalted butter
1 large onion, finely chopped
700 g (1½ lb) boned turkey thighs, skinned and cut
    into 12 mm (½ inch) cubes
125 g (4 oz) natural yogurt
2.5-5 ml (½-1 tsp) chilli powder
15 ml (1 tbsp) Ginger Paste (see page 12)
10 ml (2 tsp) Garlic Paste (see page 12)

10 ml (2 tsp) ground coriander
10 ml (2 tsp) ground cumin
5 ml (1 tsp) ground turmeric
5 ml (1 tsp) salt, or to taste
225 ml (8 fl oz) freshly squeezed orange juice, strained
5 ml (1 tsp) sugar
30 ml (2 tbsp) chopped fresh coriander leaves

1. Preheat a karahi (Balti pan) for a few seconds and add the ghee or butter. When hot, but not smoking, add the onion and stir-fry for 6-7 minutes, until it is soft and just beginning to brown.

2. Add the turkey, yogurt, chilli powder, ginger, garlic, coriander, cumin and turmeric. Reduce the heat to low, stir and mix well. Cover the karahi with a lid or a piece of foil and simmer for 25-30 minutes. (If using cooked turkey, add only the spices to the fried onion and not the turkey or the yogurt. Stir-fry the spices for 1 minute, then add the cooked meat and the yogurt. Stir-fry for 2 minutes, omit step 3 and proceed to step 4.)

3. Increase the heat to high, remove the lid and cook for 8-10 minutes, until the stock reduces to a paste-like consistency. Reduce the heat slightly, add the salt and stir-fry the meat for 4-5 minutes.

4. Reduce the heat to medium and stir in the orange juice and sugar. Cook for 2-3 minutes. Stir in the chopped coriander leaves and serve at once.

Preparation time: 20 minutes
Cooking time: 40-45 minutes

Serve with Tala hua Chawal (see page 103) and Bandgobi aur Gajjar ka Raita (see page 117).

Suitable for freezing.

Murgh Korma Shahi

(Royal Braised Chicken)
Serves 4

Korma is the Indian term for braised meat. The meat or poultry is cooked in a tightly closed pot until all the liquid evaporates, leaving only the ghee or oil used to cook the meat. The recipe, although of Mogul origin, has numerous regional variations. I have adapted this recipe for Balti cooking.

700 g (1½ lb) boned chicken thighs or breast,
   skinned and cut into 5 cm (2 inch) pieces
75 g (3 oz) natural yogurt
2.5 ml (½ tsp) ground turmeric
15 ml (1 tbsp) Ginger Paste (see page 12)
15 ml (1 tbsp) Garlic Paste (see page 12)
5 ml (1 tsp) salt
50 g (2 oz) raw unsalted cashew nuts
150 ml (¼ pint) single cream
50 g (2 oz) ghee or unsalted butter
2.5 ml (½ tsp) onion seeds (kalonji)

2.5 ml (½ tsp) fennel seeds
1 large onion, finely sliced
15 ml (1 tbsp) ground coriander
5 ml (1 tsp) ground cumin
2.5 ml (½ tsp) chilli powder, or to taste
15 ml (1 tbsp) tomato purée
300 ml (½ pint) warm water
2.5 ml (½ tsp) Balti Garam Masala (see page 10)
15 ml (1 tbsp) fresh chopped mint leaves or
   2.5 ml (½ tsp) dried mint
45 ml (3 tbsp) chopped fresh coriander leaves

1. Place the chicken, yogurt, turmeric and half the ginger, garlic and half the salt in a large mixing bowl and mix thoroughly. Cover and leave to marinate in the refrigerator for 4-6 hours or overnight. Remove from the refrigerator 30 minutes before cooking.

2. Put the cashew nuts and cream in a blender and add 45-60 ml (3-4 tbsp) water. Blend to a smooth purée and set aside.

3. Preheat a karahi (Balti pan) over a medium heat and add the ghee or butter. When hot, but not smoking, add the onion and fennel seeds and let them sizzle for a few seconds. Add the remaining ginger and garlic and stir-fry for 1 minute.

4. Add the onion and stir-fry for 6-7 minutes, until it is soft and just beginning to colour, then add the ground coriander and cumin. Stir-fry for 1 minute.

5. Add the marinated chicken and all the marinade. Increase the heat to high and stir-fry the chicken for 4-5 minutes, or until it loses its pink colour.

6. Add the chilli powder, tomato purée and the remaining salt. Stir-fry for 2-3 minutes. Add the warm water and cook for a further 3-4 minutes, stirring frequently.

7. Add the cashew and cream mixture, garam masala, mint and coriander leaves. Stir-fry for 2-3 minutes and serve.

Preparation time: 15-20 minutes, plus marinating time
Cooking time: 20 minutes

Serve with Sada Pulao or Sheermal (see page 104 or 110)

Suitable for freezing.

Murgh Korma Shahi

Zaffrani Murgh Musallam

(Saffron-flavoured Stuffed Chicken)
Serves 4

For the marinade:
2.5 ml (½ tsp) saffron strands, pounded
15 ml (1 tbsp) hot milk
1.35 kg (3 lb) oven-ready chicken
50 g (2 oz) natural yogurt
10 ml (2 tsp) Ginger Paste (see page 12)
10 ml (2 tsp) Garlic Paste (see page 12)
2.5 ml (½ tsp) ground nutmeg
2.5 ml (½ tsp) ground cardamom
2.5 ml (½ tsp) ground white pepper
2.5 ml (½ tsp) salt
For the stuffing:
30 ml (2 tbsp) sunflower, corn or vegetable oil
5 ml (1 tsp) shahi jeera (royal cumin)
1 small onion, finely chopped
1 fresh green chilli, seeded and chopped
10 ml (2 tsp) Ginger Paste (see page 12)
10 ml (2 tsp) Garlic Paste (see page 12)

225 g (8 oz) lean minced lamb
5 ml (1 tsp) ground coriander
2.5 ml (½ tsp) ground cumin
2.5 ml (½ tsp) ground turmeric
2.5 ml (½ tsp) paprika
1.25 ml (¼ tsp) chilli powder
15 ml (1 tbsp) tomato purée
125 ml (4 fl oz) single cream
15 ml (1 tbsp) chopped fresh mint leaves or 5 ml
   (1 tsp) dried mint
45 ml (3 tbsp) chopped fresh coriander leaves
5 ml (1 tsp) Balti Garam Masala (see page 10)
25 g (1 oz) butter, melted
15 ml (1 tbsp) besan (gram or chick pea flour)
1.25 ml (¼ tsp) chilli powder
To garnish:
lettuce leaves, raw onion rings, lemon wedges
   and whole fresh green chillies

1. Soak the saffron in the hot milk and set aside. Skin the chicken and trim off the excess fat. Remove the oil sac, tips from the legs and wings. Lay the chicken on a board and make three deep incisions on each breast and two similar incisions on the inner legs and two on the inner thighs. Repeat on the outer legs and thighs
2. Mix all the ingredients for the marinade including the steeped saffron. Put the chicken in a large bowl, pour the marinade over it and rub in with your fingers, making sure you work it into the incisions. Refrigerate for 24 hours. Bring to room temperature before cooking. Meanwhile, make the stuffing. Preheat a karahi (Balti pan) over a medium heat and add the oil. When hot, but not smoking, add the shahi jeera, stir once and add the onion, green chilli, ginger and garlic. Stir-fry for 4- minutes, until the onion is soft and beginning to colour.
3. Add the mince and stir-fry for 3 minutes, then add the ground coriander, cumin, turmeric, paprika and chilli powder. Stir-fry for 1 minute and add the tomato purée and cream. Stir-fry for a further minute. Add the mint, 30 ml (2 tbsp) of the coriander leaves and half the garam masala. Stir-fry for 30 seconds and remove from the heat. Allow the mince to cool. Preheat the oven to 180°C (350°F) Mark 4.
4. Spoon the stuffing into the stomach cavity, the neck end and all the incisions in the chicken. Place the chicken in a covered roasting dish. If you do not have one, cover the roasting tin with foil making sure it does not touch the chicken. Cook in the centre of the oven for 1 hour, then reduce temperature to 160°C (325°F) Mark 3 and cook for a further 30 minutes. Remove the lid or foil and cook for a further 30 minutes, basting frequently with the pan juices and the melted butter.
5. Transfer the chicken to a serving dish. Split it right down the middle so that the stuffing is visible. Surround the chicken with lettuce leaves, raw onion rings, lemon wedges and whole fresh green chillies.
6. Strain the stock and make it up to 300 ml (½ pint) with water. Blend the besan with a little water and stir it into the stock. Place over a medium heat and cook, stirring constantly, until the stock has thickened. Stir in the remaining coriander leaves and garam masala and cook for 1 minute. Serve the sauce separately.

Preparation time: 30-40 minutes, plus marinating time
Cooking time: 2 hours

Serve with Sada Pulao (see page 104) and a raita.

Murgh-Saag

(Chicken with Spinach)
Serves 4

If you have always found spinach uninteresting, try this dish, it might just change your mind! The combination is wonderful, the spicing is irresistible and you have meat and vegetable in one dish!

45 ml (3 tbsp) sunflower or corn oil

5 ml (1 tsp) fennel seeds

1 large onion, finely sliced

15 ml (1 tbsp) Ginger Paste (see page 12)

10 ml (2 tsp) Garlic Paste (see page 12)

225 g (8 oz) canned chopped tomatoes including the juice

5 ml (1 tsp) ground turmeric

15 ml (1 tbsp) ground coriander

2.5 ml (½ tsp) crushed dried chillies

450 g (1 lb) chicken thighs, boned, skinned and cut into 12 mm (½ inch) cubes

40 g (1½ oz) natural yogurt

150 ml (¼ pint) warm water

5 ml (1 tsp) salt, or to taste

225 g (8 oz) fresh spinach, finely chopped, or frozen leaf spinach, thawed and drained

10 ml (2 tsp) dried fenugreek leaves (kasoori methi), stalks removed

1.25-2.5 ml (¼-½ tsp) freshly ground black pepper

2.5 ml (½ tsp) Balti Garam Masala (see page 10)

1. Preheat a karahi (Balti pan) over a medium heat and add the oil. When hot, but not smoking, add the fennel seeds and let them sizzle for 15 seconds. Add the onion and stir-fry for 5-6 minutes, or until the onion begins to colour.

2. Add the ginger and garlic and stir-fry for 1 minute, then add the tomatoes. Stir-fry for 3-4 minutes or until the tomato juice has evaporated and the oil is visible again.

3. Add the turmeric, ground coriander and crushed chillies; stir-fry for 1 minute and add the chicken. Stir-fry for 2-3 minutes, add the yogurt and stir-fry for a further 2-3 minutes.

4. Pour in the warm water and salt and stir-fry for 5 minutes. Add the spinach and stir-fry for 4-5 minutes. Stir in the fenugreek leaves, black pepper and garam masala. Stir-fry for 1-2 minutes, then serve.

Preparation time: 25-30 minutes
Cooking time: 25-30 minutes

Serve with Balti Naan (see page 108) or any other Indian bread accompanied by Seb ki Chutney (see page 116) or a raita.

Suitable for freezing only if fresh spinach is used.

Kadhai Murgh

(Karahi Chicken)
Serves 4-6

This is the original karahi recipe which inspired the birth of an entirely new cuisine known as 'karahi cuisine' which is now known as 'Balti cuisine' in the UK. This style of cooking has been popularised in Pakistani-owned restaurants, Baltistan having become part of Pakistan after the partition of India in 1947.

700 g (1½ lb) chicken thighs, skinned and cut into
   2.5 cm (1 inch) cubes
10 ml (2 tsp) Ginger Paste (see page 12)
10 ml (2 tsp) Garlic Paste (see page 12)
75 g (3 oz) natural yogurt
50 g (2 oz) ghee or unsalted butter
1 large onion, finely chopped
2.5 ml (½ tsp) crushed dried red chillies
5 ml (1 tsp) ground turmeric

15 ml (1 tbsp) ground coriander
425 g (15 oz) canned chopped tomatoes with the juice
150 ml (¼ pint) warm water
5 ml (1 tsp) salt, or to taste
10 ml (2 tsp) dried fenugreek leaves (kasoori methi),
   stalks removed
5 ml (1 tsp) Balti Garam Masala (see page 10)
30 ml (2 tbsp) chopped fresh coriander leaves
3-4 whole fresh green chillies

1. Put the chicken in a large mixing bowl and add half the ginger, half the garlic and all the yogurt. Stir and mix thoroughly, cover the bowl and leave to marinate for 1-2 hours. It can be left overnight in the refrigerator, but remove it 30 minutes before cooking.

2. Preheat a karahi (Balti pan) over a medium heat and melt the ghee or butter; if using butter, take care not to overheat it. Add the onion and stir-fry for 8-10 minutes, until it begins to colour.

3. Add the crushed chillies and the remaining ginger and garlic, stir-fry for 1 minute, then add the turmeric and ground coriander and stir-fry for 30 seconds.

4. Add the tomatoes and cook for 6-8 minutes, or until the tomato juices have evaporated and the fat separates from the spice paste.

5. Add the chicken and increase the heat to high. Stir-fry for 4-5 minutes and add the warm water and salt. Bring to the boil, reduce the heat to medium-low and cook for 10-15 minutes, or until the sauce has thickened and the chicken is tender. Add the fenugreek leaves, garam masala, coriander leaves and fresh chillies. Cook for 1-2 minutes and serve.

Preparation time: 15 minutes, plus marinating time
Cooking time: 35-40 minutes

Serve with Balti Naan (see page 108) and Aloo-Brinjal (see page 74).

Suitable for freezing. Thaw completely before reheating.

Kadhai Murgh

Murgh Kofta Shahi

(Minced Chicken Balls in a Rich Sauce)
Serves 4

The Middle Eastern word 'kofta' means meatballs. Shahi, which means rich or royal, is generally associated with dishes cooked with cream, nuts and nut pastes. Dishes in this category, known as Mughlai (Mogul curries), were developed during the reign of the Mogul Dynasty. The Moguls originally came from the Middle East and ruled Northern and Central India until the British established their control over the sub-continent.

450 g (1lb) minced chicken or turkey
1 small onion, roughly chopped
1-2 fresh green chillies, seeded and chopped
15-20 fresh mint leaves or 2.5 ml (½ tsp) dried mint
1 egg
5 ml (1 tsp) Balti Garam Masala (see page 10)
15 ml (1 tbsp) Ginger Paste (see page 12)
15 ml (1 tbsp) Garlic Paste (see page 12)
5 ml (1 tsp) salt, or to taste
50 g (2 oz) whole milk natural yogurt
5 cm (2 inch) piece cassia bark or cinnamon stick, halved
4 green cardamom pods, the top of each pod split to release the flavour
2 black cardamom pods, the top of each pod split to release the flavour

4 cloves
2.5-5 ml (½-1 tsp) chilli powder
2.5 ml (½ tsp) ground turmeric
50 g (2 oz) ghee or unsalted butter
1 large onion, finely sliced
5 ml (1 tsp) shahi jeera (royal cumin)
5 ml (1 tsp) ground cumin
10 ml (2 tsp) ground coriander
1.25 ml (¼ tsp) ground black pepper
150 ml (¼ pint) single cream
30 ml (2 tbsp) chopped fresh coriander leaves
25 g (1 oz) unsalted, shelled pistachio nuts, lightly crushed (optional)

1. Put the minced chicken or turkey in a food processor and add the onion, green chilli, mint, egg, garam masala, 5 ml (1 tsp) each of the ginger and garlic and half the salt. Blend until you have a smooth mixture. Transfer the mixture to a bowl, cover and chill for 1-2 hours, or overnight.

2. Divide the mixture into four equal portions and make five balls out of each portion. Rotate each ball (kofta) between your palms to make them neat and smooth.

3. In a karahi (Balti pan), blend the yogurt with 300 ml (½ pint) water and add the cassia or cinnamon, both types of cardamom, cloves, chilli powder and turmeric. Place the karahi over a medium heat and bring the contents to a slow boil. Add the koftas, preferably in a single layer, cover the karahi with a lid or piece of foil and simmer for 7-8 minutes, until the koftas are firm and set. Turn them over, re-cover and simmer for a further 7-8 minutes. Remove the koftas with a slotted spoon and set aside. Strain the stock and reserve.

4. Preheat the karahi over a medium heat, add the ghee or butter and stir-fry the onions for 7-8 minutes, until they are lightly browned. Remove them with a slotted spoon and set aside.

5. Reduce the heat slightly and add the shahi jeera, then the rest of the ginger and garlic. Stir-fry for 30 seconds and add the ground cumin and coriander. Stir-fry for a further 30 seconds. Add the fried onion, koftas, the reserved stock, remaining salt, black pepper and cream. Stir until the contents begin to bubble, then cover the karahi, reduce the heat to low and simmer for 10 minutes.

6. Stir in the coriander leaves and pistachio nuts, if using, and serve.

Preparation time: 25-30 minutes
Cooking time: 35 minutes

Serve with Sheermal (see page 110) and Seb ki Chutney or Gobi Raita (see page 116 or 117).

Suitable for freezing.

Murgh-Aloo Bhoona

(Stir-fried Chicken with Potatoes)
Serves 4

Bhoona is the Indian term for cooking spices at a fairly high temperature, adding small quantities of water at regular intervals. It is the precise moment at which the water is added that is of primary importance, because this determines the final flavour of the dish. As soon as you feel the spices sticking to the bottom of the pan, add the water, then scrape and stir the contents. The secret is to allow the spices to stick, but not burn. Adding water lowers the temperature and prevents the spices from burning. This technique imparts a delicious toasted aroma to the dish. Bhoona dishes generally have a dry consistency. However, some dishes have a fair amount of sauce but the spices are cooked in the Bhoona way.

45 ml (3 tbsp) sunflower, corn or vegetable oil
1 large onion, finely chopped
10 ml (2 tsp) Ginger Paste (see page 12)
10 ml (2 tsp) Garlic Paste (see page 12)
15 ml (1 tbsp) ground cumin
10 ml (2 tsp) ground coriander
5 ml (1 tsp) ground turmeric
2.5 ml (½ tsp) chilli powder, or to taste
450 g (1 lb) boned chicken thighs, skinned and cut into
  5 cm (2 inch) cubes

5 ml (1 tsp) salt, or to taste
15 ml (1 tbsp) tomato purée
200 ml (7 fl oz) warm water
225 g (8 oz) pre-cooked potatoes, peeled and cut into
  5 cm (2 inch) cubes   .
2.5 ml (½ tsp) Balti Garam Masala (see page 10)
45 ml (3 tbsp) chopped fresh coriander leaves

1. Preheat a karahi (Balti pan) over a medium-high heat and add the oil. When hot, add the onion, ginger and garlic and stir-fry for 3-4 minutes. Add 30 ml (2 tbsp) water and stir-fry for a further 1-2 minutes. Repeat this process once more.

2. Add the ground cumin, coriander and turmeric and chilli powder. Stir-fry for 1 minute, then add 50 ml (2 fl oz) water and continue to stir-fry for a further 2 minutes, making sure you scrape up and stir the spices without letting them burn. Reduce the heat slightly, if necessary. Repeat the process of adding water, scraping and stir-frying once more.

3. Add the chicken and stir-fry for 6-7 minutes, then add the salt, tomato purée and warm water. Bring to the boil, cover the karahi with a lid or piece of foil and cook over a medium heat for 5-6 minutes.

4. Add the potatoes and reduce the heat to low, cover the karahi again and cook for 4-5 minutes. Remove the lid and simmer for 5 minutes, or until the sauce has thickened to a paste-like consistency.

5. Add the garam masala and coriander leaves, stir-fry for 1 minute, remove from the heat and serve.

Preparation time: 15 minutes
Cooking time: 30-35 minutes

Serve with Masala Roti (see page 113) and a raita, or plain boiled basmati rice and Amritsari Dhal (see page 86).

Suitable for freezing.

Badak ka Salan

(Duck Curry)
Serves 4

Although duck may not be cooked in Baltistan or in Balti restaurants, it is an excellent meat for cooking the Balti way. As with chicken, the skin and fat must be removed before cooking it. I have used duckling portions for this recipe, which comes straight from my family kitchen. If you use duck, you need to increase the cooking time.

40 g (1½ oz) ghee
4 duckling portions, about 700 g (1½ lb), skinned and
*   fat trimmed off*
1 large onion, finely chopped
10 ml (2 tsp) Ginger Paste (see page 12)
10 ml (2 tsp) Garlic Paste (see page 12)
7.5 ml (1½ tsp) dhanna-jeera powder
5 ml (1 tsp) ground turmeric

2.5 ml (½ tsp) chilli powder, or to taste
225 g (8 oz) tomatoes, skinned and chopped, or
*   canned chopped tomatoes with the juice*
300 ml (½ pint) warm water
5 ml (1 tsp) salt, or to taste
2.5 ml (½ tsp) Balti Garam Masala (see page 10)
45 ml (3 tbsp) chopped fresh coriander leaves

1. Preheat a karahi (Balti pan) briefly over a medium heat and add the ghee. When hot, add the duckling portions, one or two at a time, and brown them on both sides. Remove from the pan and set aside.
2. In the ghee remaining in the pan, stir-fry the onion, ginger and garlic for 6-7 minutes, until the onion begins to colour. Add the dhanna-jeera powder and stir-fry for 30 seconds. Add the turmeric and chilli powder and stir-fry for a further 30 seconds.
3. Add the tomatoes and stir-fry for 4-5 minutes, or until the oil separates from the spice paste.
4. Return the duckling portions to the karahi with the warm water and salt. Bring to the boil, cover the karahi and simmer for 45-50 minutes, stirring occasionally. Remove the lid, increase the heat slightly and cook for 5-6 minutes, or until the sauce thickens to a paste-like consistency.
5. Add the garam masala and coriander leaves. Stir-fry for 1 minute, then serve.

Variation: Use chicken joints instead of duckling.

Preparation time: 15-20 minutes
Cooking time: 1 hour 10 minutes

Serve with Tala hua Chawal (see page 103) and Kadhai Dhal Makhani (see page 85).

Suitable for freezing.

Badak ka Salan with Tala hua Chawal

Murgh Jeera

(Chicken with Cumin)
Serves 4

45 ml (3 tbsp) sunflower, corn or vegetable oil
5 ml (1 tsp) shahi jeera (royal cumin)
10 ml (2 tsp) Ginger Paste (see page 12)
10 ml (2 tsp) Garlic Paste (see page 12)
1 large onion, finely chopped
22.5 ml (1½ tbsp) ground cumin
5 ml (1 tsp) ground turmeric
2.5 ml (½ tsp) chilli powder, or to taste
225 g (8 oz) tomatoes, skinned and chopped, or chopped canned tomatoes with the juice

15 ml (1 tbsp) tomato purée
700 g (1½ lb) boned chicken thighs, skinned and cut into 5 cm (2 inch) cubes
5 ml (1 tsp) salt, or to taste
5 cm (2 inch) piece cassia bark or cinnamon stick, halved
4 green cardamom pods, the top of each pod split to release the flavour
225 ml (8 fl oz) warm water
45 ml (3 tbsp) chopped fresh coriander leaves

1. Preheat a karahi (Balti pan) over a medium heat and add the oil. When hot, but not smoking, add the shahi jeera and let it sizzle for 15 seconds, then add the ginger and garlic. Stir-fry for 30 seconds.
2. Add the onion and stir-fry for 6-7 minutes, until the onion begins to colour slightly.
3. Add the cumin, turmeric and chilli powder and stir-fry for 30 seconds. Add the tomatoes and tomato purée, stir-fry for 3-4 minutes, then add the chicken, salt, cassia or cinnamon, cardamom and warm water. Bring to the boil, cover the karahi with a lid or piece of foil and reduce the heat to low. Simmer for 15-20 minutes.
4. Increase the heat to medium, add the coriander leaves, stir-fry for 1-2 minutes, then serve.

Preparation time: 15-20 minutes
Cooking time: 30 minutes

Murgh Tikka Makhani

(Chicken Tikka in a Butter Sauce)
Serves 4

25 g (1 oz) unsalted butter
2.5 ml (½ tsp) onion seeds (kalonji)
2.5 ml (½ tsp) shahi jeera (royal cumin)
2.5 ml (½ tsp) Ginger Paste (see page 12)
2.5 ml (½ tsp) Garlic Paste (see page 12)
1.25 ml (¼ tsp) ground nutmeg

1.25 ml (¼ tsp) ground cardamom
350 ml (12 fl oz) Makhani Gravy (see page 13)
700 g (1½ lb) cooked Murgh Tikka (see page 69)
100 ml (4 fl oz) single cream
2.5 ml (½ tsp) dried mint
15 g (½ oz) chopped fresh coriander leaves

1. Preheat a karahi (Balti pan) over a medium heat for a few seconds. Reduce the heat to low and add the butter. When hot, but not smoking, add the onion seeds and shahi jeera and stir-fry for 15 seconds.
2. Add the ginger and garlic and stir-fry until they are lightly browned, then stir in the nutmeg and cardamom. Stir once and add the gravy and cooked Murgh Tikka. Bring to a slow simmer and cook gently for 2-3 minutes. Stir in the cream and mint and simmer for 2-3 minutes. Stir in the coriander leaves and serve.

Variation: Use Malai Seekh (see page 64) instead of Murgh Tikka.

Preparation time: 10 minutes, plus cooking the Makhani Gravy and Murgh Tikka
Cooking time: 8-10 minutes

Murgh Kalia Kesari

(Chicken with Saffron)
Serves 4

'Kalia' is a type of curry for which the base can be either milk or water combined with other ingredients to enrich it. Kesari means 'with saffron'. This recipe is of Mogul origin, a significant influence on Balti cooking.

700 g (1½ lb) boned chicken thighs, skinned and
   cut into 5 cm (2 inch) cubes
10 ml (2 tsp) Ginger Paste (see page 12)
10 ml (2 tsp) Garlic Paste (see page 12)
5 ml (1 tsp) ground fennel
10 ml (2 tsp) ground cumin
2.5-5 ml (½-1 tsp) crushed dried chillies
1 large onion, finely sliced
125 g (4 oz) whole milk natural yogurt
4 cloves

4 green cardamom pods, the top of each pod
   split to release the flavour
5 cm (2 inch) pieces cassia bark or cinnamon sticks
25 g (1 oz) ghee or unsalted butter
50 g (2 oz) ground almonds
2.5 ml (½ tsp) saffron strands, pounded
300 ml (½ pint) full cream milk
2.5 ml (½ tsp) Balti Garam Masala (see page 10)
1-2 fresh green chillies, seeded and cut into julienne
   strips

1. Put the chicken, ginger, garlic, fennel, cumin, crushed chillies, onion, yogurt, cloves, cardamom and cinnamon into a karahi (Balti pan) and place it over a medium heat. Stir until the contents begin to sizzle. Reduce the heat to low, cover the karahi with a lid or piece of foil and cook the chicken in its own juices for 20-25 minutes, stirring occasionally.
2. Remove the lid and increase the heat to high. Continue cooking until the liquid is reduced to a thick batter-like consistency, stirring frequently.
3. Add the ghee and butter and stir-fry the chicken for 3-4 minutes, or until the fat surfaces on the spice paste, then add the ground almonds and saffron. Stir-fry for 1 minute, then stir in the milk and bring to the boil. Reduce the heat to very low and simmer, uncovered, for 5 minutes.
4. Add the garam masala and fresh chillies, stir and cook for 1 minute, then serve.

Preparation time: 15 minutes
Cooking time: 30 minutes

Serve with Balti Naan (see page 108) and Bandgobi aur Gajjar ka Raita (see page 117).

Suitable for freezing.

FISH AND SHELLFISH

Outside the polar regions, the Balti region has the world's longest glaciers. The mountains range in height from 7,000 metres to 9,000 metres above sea level, giving the area its nickname 'The Roof of the World'. Fish may seem to be an unlikely food item in this rugged and elevated region; but Baltistan has been blessed with the mighty river Indus which flows right through the land. The Indus has several tributaries and the area is dotted with large lakes. I was born and brought up in the eastern foothills of the Himalayas, which is latticed by rivers and lakes with an abundance of fresh water fish, and fish was on the family menu every day.

Jhinga-Khumb Jhal Frazi

(Prawns Stir-fried with Mushrooms)
Serves 4

I usually use frozen cooked prawns for this recipe, but you can use fresh prawns — simply increase the cooking time by a few minutes.

45 ml (3 tbsp) sunflower or corn oil
2.5 ml (½ tsp) black mustard seeds
2.5 ml (½ tsp) onion seeds (kalonji)
5 ml (1 tsp) fennel seeds
1 medium onion, finely chopped
1-2 fresh green chillies, seeded and sliced
10 ml (2 tsp) Ginger Paste (see page 12)
10 ml (2 tsp) Garlic Paste (see page 12)
15 ml (1 tbsp) ground coriander
5 ml (1 tsp) ground cumin
1.25-2.5 ml (¼-½ tsp) chilli powder

2.5 ml (½ tsp) ground turmeric
200 g (7 oz) canned chopped tomatoes with the juice
15 ml (1 tbsp) tomato purée
225 g (8 oz) large open mushrooms, sliced
5 ml (1 tsp) salt, or to taste
125 ml (4 fl oz) warm water
400 g (14 oz) shelled fresh or cooked peeled prawns, thawed and drained
1.25 ml (¼ tsp) Balti Garam Masala (see page 10)
30 ml (2 tbsp) chopped fresh coriander leaves

1. Preheat a karahi (Balti pan) for a few seconds and add the oil. When hot, but not smoking, add the mustard seeds and as soon as they pop add the onion and fennel seeds. Stir-fry for 15 seconds, then add the onion and fresh chillies. Stir-fry for 5-6 minutes, or until the onion is soft and just beginning to colour.
2. Reduce the heat to low and add the ginger, garlic, ground coriander, cumin, chilli powder and turmeric. Stir-fry for 1 minute. Add the tomatoes and tomato purée. Increase the heat to medium and stir-fry for 3-4 minutes, or until oil separates from the spice paste. Add the mushrooms, salt and water. Stir-fry over high heat for 2-3 minutes and add the prawns. Stir-fry for 4-5 minutes, if fresh or 2 minutes, if frozen. Add the garam masala and fresh coriander, stir-fry for 2 minutes and serve.

Preparation time: 15-20 minutes
Cooking time: 15-20 minutes

Serve with Balti Naan (see page 108) and any chutney.

Suitable for freezing only if fresh prawns are used.

Jhinga-Khumb Jhal Frazi with Tala hua Chawal

Kadhai Jhinga

(Balti Prawns)
Serves 4

Although I am accustomed to the flavour and texture of sweet, warm water prawns, I find the North Atlantic prawns quite acceptable for cooking the Indian way. Since they are sold ready cooked, they only need to be warmed through in the sauce. Frozen prawns also work well if you thaw and drain them first. If you can get large, warm water prawns, use them – they are delicious! As they are sold raw, you will need to cook them for a few minutes, usually 8-10 minutes is enough. For this recipe, however, I have used cooked, peeled prawns.

45 ml (3 tbsp) sunflower, corn or vegetable oil
1 cm (¾ inch) piece fresh root ginger, peeled and cut
    into julienne strips
1 large onion, finely chopped
10 ml (2 tsp) Garlic Paste (see page 12)
5 ml (1 tsp) dhanna-jeera powder
2.5 ml (½ tsp) ground fennel
2.5 ml (½ tsp) chilli powder, or to taste
2.5 ml (½ tsp) ground turmeric
200 g (7 oz) tomatoes, skinned and chopped, or
    chopped canned tomatoes with the juice

15 ml (1 tbsp) tomato purée
450 g (1 lb) cooked peeled prawns
5 ml (1 tsp) salt, or to taste
2.5 ml (½ tsp) dried fenugreek leaves (kasoori methi),
    stalks removed
2.5 ml (½ tsp) Balti Garam Masala (see page 10)
175 ml (6 fl oz) warm water
15 g (½ oz) chopped fresh coriander leaves

1. Preheat a karahi (Balti pan) over a medium heat for a few seconds and add the oil. When hot, add the ginger and stir-fry for 30 seconds. Add the onion and stir-fry for 7-8 minutes, until the onion is soft and just beginning to colour.
2. Add the garlic, dhanna-jeera powder, fennel, chilli powder and turmeric. Reduce the heat slightly and stir-fry for 30 seconds, then add the tomatoes and stir-fry for 4-5 minutes, or until oil surfaces on the spice paste. Add 50 ml (2 fl oz) water and stir-fry until oil floats on the surface again.
3. Add the tomato purée, prawns, salt, fenugreek leaves and garam masala. Stir-fry for 1 minute, then add the warm water. Increase the heat slightly and stir-fry for 2-3 minutes. Stir in the coriander leaves and serve.

Preparation time: 10 minutes
Cooking time: 20 minutes

Serve with Balti Naan (see page 108) and Baigan Bharta (see page 76).

Suitable for freezing if fresh prawns are used.

→*Cook's tip:* You can make delicious Prawn Pakoras with any leftovers. Simply add enough sifted besan (gram or chick pea flour) so that you have a thick paste to coat the prawns. Season with more salt and chilli powder, if necessary. Heat the oil for deep frying in a karahi over a medium heat and put in as many dessertspoonfuls of the mixture as you can in a single layer. Fry for 8-9 minutes, or until the pakoras are evenly browned. Serve with Pudina-Dhaniya ki Chutney (see page 114).

Machchi Badami

(Fish with Almonds)
Serves 4

This recipe produces fried fish with a deliciously different flavour. In my family it is known as Indian fish and chips, as my daughter will not eat it without the chip shop kind of chips! In the original recipe, river fish is used, but sea fish such as cod, haddock or halibut are equally delicious.

15 g (½ oz) chopped fresh coriander leaves
1-2 fresh green chillies, seeded and roughly chopped
15 g (½ oz) fresh root ginger, peeled and roughly chopped
15 g (½ oz) garlic cloves, peeled and roughly chopped
5 ml (1 tsp) salt, or to taste
30 ml (2 tbsp) lemon juice

40 g (1½ oz) ground almonds
1 kg (2.2 lb) fillet of cod, haddock or halibut, skinned
oil for deep frying
40 g (1½ oz) plain flour
2 eggs, beaten
75 g (3 oz) soft white breadcrumbs

1. Put the chopped coriander, fresh chillies, ginger and garlic in a blender or food processor and add the salt, lemon juice, ground almonds and 50 ml (2 fl oz) water. Purée the ingredients and set aside.

2. Wash the fish gently and pat dry with absorbent kitchen paper. To make 'sandwiches' with the fish, using the puréed ingredients as a filling, the thicker ends of the fillets need to be prepared. The tail end and any other thinner pieces are fine as they are. First cut the fillets into 7.5 cm (3 inch) pieces. Using a sharp knife, slice each thick piece into two, in just the same way as you would slice a loaf of bread. You will now have two pieces of fish which will be equal in size and shape. Sort out all similar sized and shaped pieces for the sandwiches.

3. Spread a generous 5 ml (1 tsp) of the filling on a slice of fish and cover with another piece. Make all the sandwiches the same way, dividing the filling equally between them.

4. Heat the oil in a karahi (Balti pan) or other suitable pan over a medium heat. Dust each sandwich generously with the flour, then dip in the beaten egg and roll in the breadcrumbs. Fry them in batches until golden-brown on both sides and drain on absorbent kitchen paper.

Preparation time: 25 minutes
Cooking time: 10-12 minutes

Serve as a starter with mixed salad or as a main course accompanied by plain boiled basmati rice and Amritsari Dhal (see page 86).

Suitable for freezing. Thaw completely and reheat in a preheated moderate oven for 10-12 minutes.

Overleaf: Sabzi Masala Machchi (left) and Machchi Kofta with pappadums and Tamatar au Dhaniya ki Chutney

Sabzi Masala Machchi

(Spiced Fish with Vegetables)
Serves 4

Cooking fish with vegetables is a winter-time tradition in the Northern and North Eastern territories of the Himalayas. The severe weather causes a scarcity of meat, poultry and fish, making them very expensive. In Baltistan, and other extreme northern parts, fish and vegetables are dried in the summer months so they can be used to make sustaining winter meals. This delicious combination is perfect for warming up any winter day.

1 small aubergine, about 225 g (8 oz)
450 g (1 lb) fillet of firm white fish
5 ml (1 tsp) salt, or to taste
5 ml (1 tsp) ground turmeric
15 ml (1 tbsp) lemon juice
100 ml (4 fl oz) sunflower, corn or vegetable oil
1 medium potato, about 150 g (5 oz), peeled and cut into 2.5 cm (1 inch) cubes
25 g (1 oz) plain flour
1.25 ml (¼ tsp) black mustard seeds

1.25 ml (¼ tsp) onion seeds (kalonji)
1.25 ml (¼ tsp) fennel seeds
10 ml (2 tsp) Garlic Paste (see page 12)
10 ml (2 tsp) Ginger Paste (see page 12)
5 ml (1 tsp) ground anise seeds (ajowain)
2.5 ml (½ tsp) chilli powder
175 g (6 oz) tomatoes, skinned and chopped, or canned chopped tomatoes with the juice
300 ml (½ pint) warm water
10 ml (2 tsp) chopped fresh coriander leaves

1. Peel the aubergine and cut into 5 cm (2 inch) cubes. Soak in salted water for 30 minutes, then drain and rinse in cold water.

2. Cut the fish into 5 cm (2 inch) cubes and rub in half the salt, half the turmeric and all the lemon juice. Set aside for 15-20 minutes.

3. Heat the oil in a karahi (Balti pan) over a medium-high heat and fry the potato cubes until they are well browned. Remove and drain on absorbent kitchen paper.

4. Reduce the heat to medium, dust each piece of fish in the flour and fry them until they are well browned. Remove and drain on absorbent kitchen paper.

5. Reduce the heat to low and pour off most of the oil from the karahi, leaving about 30 ml (2 tbsp). Add the mustard seeds and as soon as they pop, add the onion and fennel seeds. Stir-fry for 15 seconds, then add the garlic and ginger. Increase the heat slightly and stir-fry for 1 minute.

6. Add the ground anise, chilli powder and remaining turmeric. Stir-fry for 30 seconds and add the tomatoes. Increase the heat to medium and stir-fry the tomatoes until oil floats to the surface.

7. Add the warm water, fried potatoes and aubergine. Bring to the boil, cover the karahi with a lid or piece of foil and reduce the heat to low. Simmer for 10 minutes, or until the potatoes and aubergines are soft. Add the fish and the remaining salt. Stir gently, re-cover and simmer for 5 minutes. Carefully stir in the chopped coriander and serve.

Variation: Use cauliflower florets instead of aubergine.

Preparation time: 25 minutes
Cooking time: 25-30 minutes

Serve with plain boiled basmati rice and hot grilled or fried pappodum.

Not suitable for freezing.

→***Cook's tip:*** You can use cod or haddock steaks but, as they are quite flaky, avoid stirring them too much once you have added them to the sauce. Coley, though much under-rated, is an excellent fish to cook with spices and it holds its shape very well during cooking.

Machchi Kofta

(Spiced Fish Balls)
Serves 4

These koftas are quick and easy to make, and are very versatile. You can make them cocktail size to serve with drinks, with or without a dip, as a starter, side dish or even a main meal. I often double the quantity and freeze some for cooking later with a sauce.

2 large slices of day-old white bread, about
   100 g (4 oz)
450 g (1 lb) fillet of cod or haddock, skinned and
   roughly chopped
15 g (½ oz) fresh coriander leaves including the tender
   stalks, chopped
1 egg
5 ml (1 tsp) salt, or to taste
30 ml (2 tbsp) sunflower, corn or vegetable oil

1 onion, finely chopped
10 ml (2 tsp) Ginger Paste (see page 12)
10 ml (2 tsp) Garlic Paste (see page 12)
1-2 fresh green chillies, seeded and chopped
5 ml (1 tsp) ground anise seed (ajowain)
2.5 ml (½ tsp) chilli powder, or to taste
2.5 ml (½ tsp) Balti Garam Masala (see page 10)
oil for deep frying

1. Soak the slices of bread in cold water for 1 minute, then squeeze out all the water. Place the bread, fish, coriander, egg and salt in a food processor and blend until smooth. Transfer the mixture to a large mixing bowl and set aside.

2. Preheat a karahi (Balti pan) over a medium heat and add the oil. When hot, add the onion, ginger and garlic and stir-fry for 4-5 minutes, until the onion is soft but not brown. Add the fresh chillies, ground anise, chilli powder and garam masala. Stir-fry for 1-2 minutes, then remove from the heat and leave the mixture to cool. When cold, mix it thoroughly with the ground fish mixture and chill in the refrigerator for 1-2 hours or overnight.

3. Divide the mixture into four equal portions. Shape each portion into five balls (koftas). Heat the oil in the karahi over a medium heat until almost smoking. Fry the koftas for 6-8 minutes, until they are evenly browned. Drain on absorbent kitchen paper and serve.

Variation: For a main course, simmer the fried koftas in 450 ml (15 fl oz) Makhani Gravy (see page 13) for 4-5 minutes. Sprinkle with 2.5 ml (½ tsp) Balti Garam Masala (see page 10) and 1.25 ml (¼ tsp) chilli powder and serve with plain boiled basmati rice and Kadhai Sabzi Masala (see page 72).

Preparation time: 20 minutes, plus chilling time
Cooking time: 6-8 minutes

Serve as a starter with Tamatar aur Dhaniya ki Chutney (see page 116) and spiced pappadum.

Machchi Kalia

(Fish in a Rich Tomato and Onion Sauce)
Serves 4

This simple, but fine tasting, fish curry is one from my mother's repertoire. No special occasion meal was complete without this curry on the menu. Inspite of all the other dishes on the table, I very often ate nothing else but Machchi Kalia and plain boiled basmati rice for my entire meal. My mother used river fish, which has a firm texture and can be cooked in a sauce without flaking, but firm-fleshed sea fish can be used just as successfully.

700 g (1½ lb) fillet or steaks of firm-textured fish, such as monkfish, grey mullet or coley
30 ml (2 tbsp) lemon juice
5 ml (1 tsp) salt
5 ml (1 tsp) ground turmeric
oil for shallow frying
40 g (1½ oz) plain flour
1.25 ml (¼ tsp) freshly ground black pepper
60 ml (4 tbsp) sunflower, corn or vegetable oil
10 ml (2 tsp) sugar

1 large onion, finely chopped
15 ml (1 tbsp) Ginger Paste (see page 12)
15 ml (1 tbsp) Garlic Paste (see page 12)
2.5 ml (½ tsp) ground anise seed
5 ml (1 tsp) ground coriander
2.5 ml (½ tsp) chilli powder, or to taste
175 g (6 oz) fresh tomatoes skinned and chopped, or canned chopped tomatoes with the juice
300 ml (½ pint) warm water
45 ml (3 tbsp) chopped fresh coriander leaves

1. Skin the fish and cut into 7.5 cm (3 inch) pieces. Pour the lemon juice over it and sprinkle with half the salt and half the turmeric. Mix gently but thoroughly and set aside for 15 minutes.

2. Pour enough oil into a 23 cm (9 inch) frying pan to cover the base to a depth of about 12 mm (½ inch) and heat over a medium heat. Mix the flour and pepper together. When the oil is hot, dust each piece of fish in the seasoned flour and fry in a single layer until well browned on both sides and a light crust has formed. Drain on absorbent kitchen paper.

3. Preheat a karahi (Balti pan) over a medium heat for a few seconds and add the oil. When hot, add the sugar and allow it to brown, but watch it carefully because once it browns it can blacken quickly. As soon as the sugar is brown, add the onion, ginger and garlic and stir-fry for 7-8 minutes, until the onion is soft and just beginning to colour.

4. Add the ground anise and stir-fry for 30 seconds, then add the ground coriander and stir-fry for 1 minute. Add the chilli powder and remaining turmeric, stir-fry for 30 seconds, then add the tomatoes and stir-fry for 4-5 minutes, or until the tomato juice has evaporated, the mixture is thick and oil surfaces on the spice paste.

5. Pour in the warm water, add the remaining salt and bring to the boil. Gently add the fried fish, reduce the heat to low and simmer, uncovered, for 5-6 minutes. Stir in the coriander leaves and serve.

Variation: Use cod or haddock fillets, but arrange the fried fish in a shallow ovenproof dish in a single layer. Add the coriander leaves to the sauce and pour over the fish. Cook in the centre of a preheated oven at 180°C (350°F) Mark 4 for 8-10 minutes.

Preparation time: 25-30 minutes
Cooking time: 30 minutes

Serve with plain boiled basmati rice, accompanied by any vegetable dish.

Suitable for freezing.

Machchi Kalia

Dahi Machchi

(Fish in Yogurt)
Serves 4

Originally cooked by the 'dum' method, which is the Indian term for pot roasting, I have adapted this recipe for cooking the Balti way. The combination of yogurt and besan (gram or chick pea flour), cooked over a very low heat, produces a superb creamy sauce with a slightly nutty flavour.

700 g (1½ lb) fillet or steaks of firm fish, such as monkfish, grey mullet, or river trout
5 ml (1 tsp) ground turmeric
5 ml (1 tsp) salt, or to taste
175 g (6 oz) whole milk natural yogurt
25 g (1 oz) besan (gram or chick pea flour), sieved
100 ml (4 fl oz) sunflower, corn or vegetable oil
2 medium onions, finely sliced
25 g (1 oz) plain flour

10 ml (2 tsp) Ginger Paste (see page 12)
10 ml (2 tsp) Garlic Paste (see page 12)
2.5-5 ml (½-1 tsp) crushed dried chillies
5 ml (1 tsp) ground anise seeds (ajowain)
10 ml (2 tsp) ground coriander
150 ml (¼ pint) warm water
2-4 fresh green chillies, seeded and cut into julienne strips
2.5 ml (½ tsp) Balti Garam Masala (see page 10)
45 ml (3 tbsp) chopped fresh coriander leaves

1. Cut the fish into chunky pieces, about 7.5 cm (3 inches) square and gently rub in half the turmeric and half the salt. Set aside for 15-20 minutes.

2. Beat the yogurt and besan together until smooth, and set aside.

3. Heat the oil in a karahi (Balti pan) over a medium heat, add the onions and stir-fry until they are lightly browned. Remove with a slotted spoon and drain on absorbent kitchen paper.

4. Increase the heat slightly and allow the remaining oil to heat to smoking point. Dust each piece of fish lightly in the plain flour and fry in batches until they are browned. Drain on absorbent kitchen paper.

5. Pour off most of the oil from the karahi, leaving about 15 ml (1 tbsp). Reduce the heat to low and stir-fry the ginger and garlic for 1 minute, then add the crushed chillies, ground anise, coriander and the remaining turmeric. Stir-fry for 1 minute.

6. Add the yogurt mixture, warm water and the remaining salt. Stir once and add the fried onions and the fish. Stir very gently to mix. Cover the karahi with a lid or piece of foil, reduce the heat to very low and cook for 7-10 minutes.

7. Add the chillies, garam masala and coriander leaves. Stir gently and cook for 1-2 minutes, then serve.

Preparation time: 15 minutes
Cooking time: 20 minutes

Serve with plain boiled basmati rice and any vegetable dish or a dhal.

Not suitable for freezing.

Hara Masala ki Machchi

(Fish with Green Spices)
Serves 4

Simple, delicious and irresistible is how I would describe this recipe! Chunky pieces of fish are smothered in a coriander-based, fresh spice mix with an added nutty flavour from the besan (gram or chick pea flour).

700 g (1½ lb) fillet of cod or haddock, skinned
3 spring onions, white part only
2 large garlic cloves, peeled and roughly chopped
25 g (1 oz) fresh root ginger, peeled and roughly chopped
30 ml (2 tbsp) lemon juice
15 g (½ oz) fresh coriander leaves including the tender stalks, roughly chopped

2-4 fresh green chillies, seeded and roughly chopped
5 ml (1 tsp) salt, or to taste
75 g (3 oz) besan (gram or chick pea flour), sieved
oil for deep frying

1 Wash the fish gently under running water and pat dry with absorbent kitchen paper. Cut each fillet into 5 cm (2 inch) pieces. As the tail end is thin, this can be folded over to match the thickness of the other pieces.
2. Put all the ingredients, except the besan and oil, in a blender, add 30-45 ml (2-3 tbsp) water and blend to a smooth paste.
3. Put the fish in a large mixing bowl, pour the spice paste over it and mix gently and thoroughly with a metal spoon. Cover the bowl and leave the fish to marinate for 2-3 hours or overnight in the refrigerator.
4. Add the sieved besan and 45 ml (3 tbsp) water and mix gently until the fish is coated with the paste. Add a little more water if you find the paste is not wet enough to completely coat the fish.
5. Heat the oil in a karahi over a medium-high heat and fry the fish in batches for 2½ minutes on each side, until they are golden-brown on both sides. Drain on absorbent kitchen paper.

Preparation time: 20 minutes, plus marinating time
Cooking time: 10-15 minutes

Serve as a starter with Bandgobi aur Gajjar ka Raita (see page 117) or as a side dish with Tala hua Chawal (see page 103) and Kadhai Dhal Makhani (see page 85).

Suitable for freezing. Thaw overnight in the refrigerator and reheat in a preheated oven at 200°C (400°F) Mark 6 for 10-12 minutes.

KABABS AND TANDOORI DISHES

Kababs are believed to be a totally nomadic invention. In a nomadic life-style there was no room for subtle and skilful methods of cooking. Whatever they found during their day's hunt was put on a spit and hung over the fire to roast. In the rugged North West Frontier of India (now in Pakistan), wild life is everywhere, sheep and yak being the most prominent. The basic food of the nomads who settled in Baltistan and its surrounding areas were kababs (kababs) and roti (bread). Archaeologists in the Indus Valley site found remains of clay ovens which looked like modern-day tandoor ovens. These ovens were used to cook naan (bread) and other tandoori items, such as kababs. Tandoori cooking has now been refined and varied to a great extent. Included in this chapter are a selection of kababs and other dishes which are traditionally cooked in the tandoor, but I have adapted them for cooking in any domestic gas or electric oven. Alternatively, they are excellent for barbecuing.

Barrah Kabab

(Spiced Lamb Chops)
Serves 6

6 lamb chump or shoulder chops, total weight about
   1 kg (2.2 lb)
75 g (3 oz) natural yogurt
30 ml (2 tbsp) light malt vinegar
15 ml (1 tbsp) Ginger Paste (see page 12)
15 ml (1 tbsp) Garlic Paste (see page 12)
2.5-5 ml (½-1 tsp) crushed dried chillies
50 g (2 oz) onion, chopped
10 ml (2 tsp) Balti Garam Masala (see page 10)
5 ml (1 tsp) Tandoori Masala (see page 11)

30 ml (2 tbsp) fresh mint leaves or 5 ml (1 tsp) dried
   mint
15 g (½ oz) chopped fresh coriander leaves, including
   the tender stalks
5 ml (1 tsp) salt, or to taste
45 ml (3 tbsp) sunflower, corn or vegetable oil
To garnish:
2.5 ml (½ tsp) Tandoori Chaat Masala (see page 11),
   onion rings, lemon wedges, lettuce and cucumber

1. Prick both sides of the chops with a fork and lay them in a single layer a large shallow dish.
2. Place all the remaining ingredients, except the garnish, in a blender and process to a fine paste. Pour this marinade over the chops, then stir and lift them to make sure that the marinade is coating both sides. Cover and leave to marinate for 4-6 hours or overnight in the refrigerator. They can be left in the refrigerator for up to 48 hours. Bring them to room temperature before cooking.
3. Preheat the grill to high and remove the grid from the grill pan. Line the pan with foil and brush lightly with oil. Arrange the chops in the grill pan and cook them under the hot grill, about 12.5 cm (5 inches) below the element, for 5 minutes. Turn the chops over and cook for a further 5 minutes, then baste generously with the pan juices and reduce the heat to medium. Cook for 3-4 minutes and baste once more. Cook for a further 2-3 minutes and turn them over again. Baste generously again and continue cooking for 5-6 minutes.
4. Transfer the chops to a serving dish, sprinkle the tandoori chaat masala over them and garnish with the onion, lemon and cucumber. Serve at once.

Preparation time: 10-15 minutes, plus marinating time
Cooking time: 5-20 minutes

Barrah Kabab

Malai Seekh

(Skewered Creamy Lamb Kababs)
Makes 8

The enticing flavour of lamb with cashew nuts and cream is a favourite dish. As the cashews are ground to a paste, use cheaper cashew pieces rather than whole nuts. Broken cashew pieces are sold in most health food stores and Asian shops.

50 g (2 oz) cashew nuts or pieces
1 size 2 egg
450 g (1 lb) minced lamb
1 small onion, roughly chopped
25 g (1 oz) fresh root ginger, peeled and roughly chopped
2 small garlic cloves, peeled
2-4 fresh green chillies, seeded and roughly chopped
15 g (½ oz) coriander leaves, including the tender stalks, roughly chopped

15-20 fresh mint leaves or 5 ml (1 tsp) mint chutney
10 ml (2 tsp) ground cumin
5 ml (1 tsp) Balti Garam Masala (see page 10)
30 ml (2 tbsp) double cream
5 ml (1 tsp) salt, or to taste
30 ml (2 tbsp) vegetable or corn oil
To garnish:
onion rings, cucumber slices and lemon wedges

1. Put the cashew nuts in a food processor and blend until they have a coarse finish. Add the remaining ingredients, except the garnish, and blend until smooth. Transfer the mixture to a covered container and chill in the refrigerator for 1-2 hours. It can be left overnight in the refrigerator, if wished.
2. Preheat the grill to high. Remove the grid from the grill pan and line the pan with foil.
3. Divide the lamb mixture in half and make four equal portions from each half. Grease the palms and fingers of your hands and carefully mould each portion on to a skewer, patting and stretching it gently into a 15 cm (6 inch) long sausage shape.
4. Arrange the kababs in the grill pan and place under the hot grill, about 15 cm (6 inches) away from the element. Grill for 5 minutes, then carefully turn the kababs over and grill for a further 5 minutes.
5. Remove from the heat and carefully slide the meat off the skewers with a table knife. Transfer to a serving plate and garnish with onion rings, cucumber slices and lemon wedges.

Preparation time: 20-25 minutes, plus chilling time
Cooking time: 10 minutes

Serve as a starter or as a main course with Balti Naan or Sheermal (see page 108 or 110), any raita or chutney and Kadhai Dhal Makhani (see page 85). Alternatively, cut the kababs into about 2.5 cm (1 inch) pieces and serve with drinks.

Suitable for freezing. Thaw thoroughly and reheat in the oven at 200˚C (400˚F) Mark 6 for 5-6 minutes. Alternatively, reheat them in a covered dish in the microwave for about 45 seconds per kabab.

Reshmi Kabab

(Silky Minced Chicken Kabab)
Makes 12

A fabulous combination of ground cashew nuts, minced chicken and traditional herbs and spices, Reshmi Kababs are delicious and fairly easy to make. I have used chicken breast in this recipe, but a combination of breast and thigh meat can be used. Minced turkey can also be used. Use broken cashew pieces, available in health food shops and Asian stores, as these are cheaper than the whole ones.

50 g (2 oz) cashew nuts or pieces
700 g (1½ lb) boned and skinned chicken breast, roughly chopped
15 ml (1 tbsp) Garlic Paste (see page 12)
15 ml (1 tbsp) Ginger Paste (see page 12)
15 ml (1 tbsp) ground cumin
5 ml (1 tsp) ground fennel
7.5 ml (1½ tsp) Balti Garam Masala (see page 10)
2.5 ml (½ tsp) chilli powder

1-2 fresh green chillies, seeded and roughly chopped
25 g (1 oz) coriander leaves, including the tender stalks, roughly chopped
30 ml (2 tbsp) sunflower or corn oil
1 large egg
5 ml (1 tsp) salt, or to taste
1 small onion, roughly chopped
40 g (1½ oz) butter, melted

1. Put the cashews in the food processor and process until they have a coarse finish.
2. Add all the remaining ingredients, except the butter, and blend until smooth. Transfer the mixture to a large bowl or empty ice cream tub, cover and chill in the refrigerator for 1-2 hours, or overnight.
3. Preheat the oven to 200°C (400°F) Mark 6. Line a baking sheet with foil and brush it with oil. Have 12 skewers ready.
4. Lightly grease the palms of your hands and fingers (this will stop the mixture sticking to your hands) and divide the chicken mixture into 12 equal portions. Mould each portion on to a skewer and make a sausage shape by gently patting and stretching it to about 15 cm (6 inches) in length. Grease your hands frequently while shaping the kababs. Place the skewers on the prepared baking sheet.
5. Cook the kababs in the top of the oven for 5 minutes, then baste generously with the melted butter. Turn them over and cook for 3-4 minutes, then baste again and cook for 2-3 minutes. If you need to cook them in batches, keep the cooked ones hot by wrapping them in foil. Serve hot.

Variation: Traditionally, kababs are skewered because they are cooked in the tandoor and the skewers make it easier to handle them. It is not essential for a domestic oven, and if you find it difficult to mould them on to the skewers, simply make the mixture into sausage shapes and place them on the prepared baking sheet.

Preparation time: 25-30 minutes, plus chilling time
Cooking time: 12-15 minutes

Serve as a starter with any chutney or raita, cucumber slices and raw onion rings. They can also be cut into pieces and served as a side dish or with drinks.

Kastoori Kabab

(Fragrant Chicken Kababs)
Serves 4

700 g (1½ lb) boned chicken breast, skinned
30 ml (2 tbsp) lemon juice
30 ml (2 tbsp) natural yogurt
10 ml (2 tsp) Garlic Paste (see page 12)
10 ml (2 tsp) Ginger Paste (see page 12)
5 ml (1 tsp) chilli powder
7.5 ml (1½ tsp) Balti Garam Masala (see page 10)
15 g (½ oz) fresh coriander leaves, including the
    tender stalks, finely chopped
5 ml (1 tsp) shahi jeera (royal cumin)

salt
50 g (2 oz) besan (gram or chick pea flour),
    sieved
2.5 ml (½ tsp) ground cumin
2.5 ml (½ tsp) chilli powder
1 small egg, beaten
25 g (1 oz) unsalted butter, melted
To garnish:
sliced red onions, sliced cucumber, tomato
    wedges and lime or lemon wedges

1. Wash the chicken and pat dry. Cut into 5 cm (2 inch) cubes.
2. In a large mixing bowl, mix together the lemon juice, yogurt, garlic, ginger, chilli powder, garam masala, coriander leaves, shahi jeera and 5 ml (1 tsp) salt. Add the chicken and stir to mix thoroughly. Cover the container and leave to marinate for 4-6 hours, or overnight in the refrigerator. Remove from the refrigerator 30 minutes before cooking.
3. Preheat the oven to 200°C (400°F) Mark 6. Remove grid from the grill pan and line the pan with foil.
4. Mix the besan with the cumin, chilli powder and 1.25 ml (¼ tsp) salt. Stir this mixture into the marinated chicken and mix well. Add the beaten egg and mix until the chicken is well coated with the mixture.
5. Thread the chicken on to skewers, leaving a small gap between each piece. Place the prepared skewers on the grill pan and cook in the upper part of the oven for 5 minutes. Baste with some of the melted butter and cook for a further 3-4 minutes. Turn the skewers over, baste with the remaining butter and cook for 2-3 minutes. Garnnish with red onions, cucumber, tomato and lime or lemon and serve.

Preparation time: 20-25 minutes, plus marinating time
Cooking time: 10 minutes

Tandoori Machchi

(Fish Tandoori Style)
Serves 4

Tandoori fish is traditionally made with India's most popular fish, pomfret, a firm-fleshed tender fish, similar to sole and plaice. For this recipe I have used lemon sole.

2 large or 4 small lemon soles, about 1 kg
    (2.2 lb) in total
5 ml (1 tsp) salt, or to taste
22.5 ml (1½ tbsp) lemon juice
75 g (3 oz) natural yogurt
15 ml (1 tbsp) Ginger Paste (see page 12)
15 ml (1 tbsp) Garlic Paste (see page 12)
about 5 ml (1 tsp) chilli powder

5 ml (1 tsp) ground anise (ajwain)
75 ml (3 fl oz) single cream
15 ml (1 tbsp) gram flour (chick pea flour or
    besan), sieved
50 ml (2 fl oz) sunflower, corn or vegetable oil
To garnish:
shredded lettuce, cucumber, tomato and lemon
    wedges, red onion rings

1. Scale the fish and trim the fins. Wash gently and dry thoroughly with absorbent kitchen paper. Make deep incisions across the fish at 4 cm (1½ inch) intervals. Turn the fish over and make similar incisions. Sprinkle the salt all over the fish. Rub the lemon juice over both sides of the fish, then set them aside for 30 minutes.

2. Mix together the remaining ingredients, except the oil, in a bowl and beat with a fork until smooth. Pour the marinade over the fish and rub it in well, making sure you rub inside the incisions as well as filling the incisions with the marinade. Cover and leave to marinate in the refrigerator for 2-4 hours, or overnight. Bring it to room temperature before cooking.

3. Preheat the grill to medium and remove the grid from the grill pan. Line the pan with foil and brush with a little of the oil. Put the fish on the prepared pan and cook about 12.5 cm (5 inches) below the element for 3-4 minutes, then brush with some of the oil. Cook for a further 3-4 minutes, then turn the fish over. Cook for 3-4 minutes and baste with the remaining oil. Cook for a further 3-4 minutes. Garnish and serve at once.

Preparation time: 20 minutes, plus standing and marinating time
Cooking time: 12-15 minutes

Tandoori Aloo

(Tandoori-style Potatoes)
Serves 4-6

700 g (1½ lb) old potatoes, peeled and cut into 2.5 cm (1 inch) dice
60 ml (4 tbsp) sunflower or corn oil
5 ml (1 tsp) salt, or to taste
7.5 ml (1½ tsp) ground cumin
10 ml (2 tsp) Garlic Paste (see page 12)
5 ml (1 tsp) dry ginger powder (santh)

5 ml (1 tsp) Tandoori Masala (see page 11)
7.5 ml (1½ tsp) lemon juice
2.5 ml (½ tsp) chilli powder (optional)
15 ml (1 tbsp) dried fenugreek leaves (kasoori methi), stalks removed
25 g (1 oz) besan (gram or chick pea flour), sieved
30 ml (2 tbsp) chopped fresh coriander leaves

1. In a roasting tin, mix together all the ingredients except the coriander. Cover and set aside for 1-2 hours.

2. Preheat the oven to 190°C (375°F) Mark 5. Cook the potatoes in the centre of the oven for 20 minutes. Stir thoroughly and cook for a further 8-10 minutes. Remove the tin from the oven and stir in the coriander leaves. Serve at once.

Preparation time: 10-15 minutes
Cooking time: 30 minutes

Tandoori Murgh

(Tandoori Chicken)
Serves 4

This well-known and much loved tandoori dish is one of the easiest to make. Once you mixed the tandoori masala and marinated the chicken, all you have to do is put the chicken in the oven! I like to roast the whole bird, but you can use joints, if preferred, and reduce the cooking time to about 30 minutes.

1.75 kg (3½ lb) oven-ready chicken
30 ml (2 tbsp) lemon juice
5 ml (1 tsp) salt, or to taste
125 g (4 oz) natural yogurt
25 g (1 oz) piece fresh root ginger, peeled and roughly
  chopped
25 g (1oz) garlic cloves, peeled and roughly chopped
50 g (2 oz) onion, chopped

10 ml (2 tsp) Tandoori Masala (see page 11)
2.5 ml (½ tsp) chilli powder (optional)
40 g (1½ oz) unsalted butter, melted
2.5 ml (½ tsp) Tandoori Chaat Masala (see page 11)
To garnish:
shredded crisp lettuce leaves and red onion,
  cucumber and tomato slices

1. Skin the chicken, wash and pat dry. To enable the spices to penetrate deep inside it, lay the chicken on a board and make three deep incisions on each breast at right angles to the spine. Make two similar incisions on the inner legs and two on the inner thighs. Turn the chicken over and repeat the process on the other leg and thigh. Finally, make two or three incisions on both sides of the wings. If using chicken joints, make incisions in the same way on both sides of them.

2. Pour the lemon juice over the chicken and sprinkle with the salt. Using fingers, rub the lemon juice and salt into the chicken, making sure the mixture goes into the incisions. Set aside for 30 minutes.

3. Place the remaining ingredients, except the butter, tandoori chaat masala and garnish, in a blender or food processor and blend to a fine purée. Put the chicken in a large bowl or other suitable container and pour the marinade over it. Rub it in with your fingers, making sure the marinade goes into the slits and the stomach cavity. Turn the chicken over so that it is breast side down. Cover the bowl and leave the chicken to marinate in the refrigerator for 24-36 hours. Remove from the refrigerator 1 hour before cooking.

4. Preheat the oven to 220°C (425°F) Mark 7. Line a roasting tin with foil and place the chicken on its back in the tin. Pour over any remaining marinade and cook in the centre of the oven for 20 minutes for whole chicken and 12-15 minutes for joints. Reduce the temperature to 200°C (400°F) Mark 6 and baste the chicken with the pan juices. Cook for a further 20 minutes for a whole bird or 10 minutes for joints.

5. Baste the chicken generously with some of the melted butter as well as the pan juices. Cook for a further 20 minutes, basting with melted butter and pan juices every 5 minutes. Chicken joints will only need 5 minutes. Transfer to a serving dish and garnish with shredded lettuce and onion, cucumber and tomato slices. Carve the bird at the table. Remove the leg joints first, then the two breast joints.

Preparation time: 30 minutes, plus marinating time
Cooking time: 1 hour

Serve as a starter with salad or as a main meal with Sheermal (see page 110) and Dum Aloo Kashmiri (see page 73). Cut the joints into smaller pieces to serve as a starter. The rest of the meat can be removed and, together with any leftovers, can to used to make a delicious Makhani Murgh (see page 32).

Suitable for freezing. Thaw completely before reheating. Joints can be reheated in the centre of a preheated oven at 190°C (375°F) Mark 5, wrapped in a double thickness of foil for 20 minutes in the centre of the oven. To freeze the whole bird, follow the recipe to the end of step 4, cool the chicken and wrap in foil with all the pan juices, then freeze. Thaw completely, then proceed with the recipe from step 5 and extend the time by a further 20 minutes.

Murgh Tikka

(Chicken Tikka)
Serves 4

This tasty dish has become popular the length and breadth of Britain. A traditional tandoori dish, it is easy to cook in a domestic oven. The choice of meat is entirely a matter of personal preference. You can use breast or thigh, though I personally find thigh meat more flavoursome and succulent than breast meat.

700 g (1½ lb) boned, skinless chicken breast or thigh, cut into 5 cm (2 inch) cubes
22.5 ml (1½ tbsp) lemon juice
5 ml (1 tsp) salt
5 ml (1 tsp) sugar
75 g (3 oz) natural yogurt
75 ml (3 fl oz) single cream
15 ml (1 tbsp) Ginger Paste (see page 12)
10 ml (2 tsp) Garlic Paste (see page 12)
10 ml (2 tsp) ground cumin
5 ml (1 tsp) ground coriander
5 ml (1 tsp) Balti Garam Masala (see page 10)

5 ml (1 tsp) ground turmeric
2.5 ml (½ tsp) chilli powder
15 ml (1 tbsp) besan (gram or chick pea flour), sieved
oil for brushing
40 g (1½ oz) butter, melted
To garnish:
raw onion rings, lemon wedges, tomato wedges, fresh green chillies, seeded and slit lengthways, 2.5 ml (½ tsp) Tandoori Chaat Masala (see page 11)

1. Put the chicken in a mixing bowl and add the lemon juice, salt and sugar. Mix thoroughly and set aside for 30 minutes.
2. Beat the yogurt and cream together in a bowl until smooth, then add the remaining ingredients, except the oil, butter and garnish. Pour the marinade over the chicken and stir to distribute and mix well. Cover and leave to marinate in a cool place for 3-4 hours, or overnight in the refrigerator. Once marinated, it can be left in the refrigerator for up to 48 hours.
3. Preheat the grill to high. Remove the grid from the grill pan and line with a piece of foil, then brush with a little oil. Thread the chicken on to skewers, leaving a slight gap between each piece. Place the skewered chicken in the prepared grill pan and cook approximately 10 cm (4 inches) below the element for 5 minutes. Baste generously with some of the melted butter, reduce heat slightly and cook for a further 5 minutes. Turn the skewers over and brush with the remaining butter. Cook for 4-5 minutes, then remove from the heat.
4. Allow to rest for 2-3 minutes, then remove the chicken from the skewers and place on a serving dish. Garnish with the onion, lemon, tomatoes and chillies, and sprinkle the tandoori chaat masala over the top.

Preparation time: 20-25 minutes, plus marinating time
Cooking time: 10-12 minutes

Serve with Pudina-Dhaniya ki Chutney (see page 114) and Masala Roti (see page 113).

Suitable for freezing.

→**Cook's tip:** Mix cooked Murgh Tikka with Sada Pulao (see page 105) to make a delicious Chicken Tikka Pulao. Garnish with fried onions and toasted flaked almonds, and serve with Sabzi Masala Malai (see page 82).

Peshawari Raan

(Peshawar-style Leg of Lamb)
Serves 4-6

The word 'raan' means leg of lamb. First popularised by the Mongolian warrior Chengiz Khan (1162-1227 AD), the legendary dish Chengezi Raan has today been adapted to several styles of cooking. Peshawari Raan is one of the most popular among them. The leg of lamb is first marinated, then simmered until tender and finally roasted in the tandoor. A gas or electric oven is quite capable of cooking this to perfection. Yogurt is not generally used in the marinade, but I like the tenderising effect it has on the meat.

3 kg (6 lb 10 oz) leg of lamb, any membrane and
   excess fat removed
60 ml (4 tbsp) light malt vinegar
75 g (3 oz) natural yogurt
7.5 ml (1½ tsp) salt, or to taste
5-7.5 ml (1-1½ tsp) chilli powder
30 ml (2 tbsp) Ginger Paste (see page 12)

30 ml (2 tbsp) Garlic Paste (see page 12)
10 ml (2 tsp) Balti Garam Masala (see page 10)
5 ml (1 tsp) Tandoori Masala (see page 11)
To garnish:
5 ml (1 tsp) Tandoori Chaat Masala (see page 11), red
   onion rings, cucumber slices, tomato slices and
   lemon wedges

1. Lay the leg of lamb on a board and make small, deep incisions on both sides. They should be short, deep and scattered all over the leg to allow the flavours to penetrate. Transfer the lamb to a large, deep dish.

2. Mix all the remaining ingredients, except the garnish, together and pour half this marinade over the lamb. Rub it into the meat, making sure it goes into the incisions. Turn the leg over and repeat the process with the remaining marinade. Cover the dish, making sure it is well sealed and leave to marinate in the refrigerator for 24-36 hours. Bring to room temperature before cooking, this will take about 2 hours.

3. Preheat the oven to 180°C (350°F) Mark 4. Place the marinated leg in a deep roasting tin. If your roasting tin is shallow, you will need to check the water level during cooking and add more water if necessary.

4. Scrape any remaining marinade from the dish and spoon it over the meat. Pour 300-600 ml (10 fl oz-1 pint) water into the roasting tin, but not over the meat. Cover and seal tightly with foil and cook in the centre of the oven for 1 hour. Turn the leg over, re-cover and cook for a further 1 hour.

5. Remove the foil and baste the meat generously with the pan juices. Return it to the oven for 10 minutes, then baste with half the melted butter and cook for 6-8 minutes. Carefully turn the meat over, baste with the remaining butter and cook for a further 6-8 minutes. If any juice remains in the pan, spoon it over the meat and it will be absorbed very quickly. Do this on both sides if necessary.

6. Divide the tandoori chaat masala into three equal parts and sprinkle one part over the leg of lamb. Turn the meat over and transfer it to a large serving dish. Sprinkle with the second quantity of chaat masala and garnish with the onions, cucumber, tomatoes and lemon wedges. Sprinkle the last third of chaat masala all over the salad ingredients and serve at once.

Preparation time: 20-25 minutes, plus marinating time
Cooking time: 2 hours 25 minutes

→**Cook's tip:** If you have any leftovers from this dish, turn this into a delicious lamb pulao. Simply reheat it with a little water in a karahi (Balti pan) and mix with Sada Pulao (see page 104). Garnish with fried onions and serve with a raita and fried pappadums.

Peshawari Raan

VEGETABLE DISHES

Although Balti cuisine is predominantly meat based it does not mean that vegetables are excluded altogether. In the fertile valley of the river Indus, an enormous range of vegetables are grown in the summer. Kashmir has unique floating gardens where cucumbers, tomatoes, mint and water melons are grown. Aubergines, mushrooms, sweetcorn and a whole host of other vegetables are dried and stored for the long winter months. Kashmir is the only part of India where mushrooms grow abundantly, but cultivated mushrooms are now available in many parts of India.

Kadhai Sabzi Masala

(Balti Spiced Vegetables)
Serves 4-6

700 g (1½ lb) whole green beans, cut into 2.5 cm
  (1 inch) pieces
700 g (1½ lb) old potatoes, peeled and cut into 2.5 cm
  (1 inch) cubes
45 ml (3 tbsp) sunflower or corn oil
5 ml (1 tsp) fennel seeds
two 5 cm (2 inch) pieces cassia bark or cinnamon
  sticks, broken up
1 medium onion, finely sliced
5 ml (1 tsp) Ginger Paste (see page 12)
5 ml (1 tsp) Garlic Paste (see page 12)
10 ml (2 tsp) ground coriander

5 ml (1 tsp) ground cumin
5 ml (1 tsp) ground turmeric
2.5 ml (½ tsp) chilli powder, or to taste
150 g (5 oz) chopped canned tomatoes including the
  juice
5 ml (1 tsp) salt, or to taste
5 ml (1 tsp) dried fenugreek leaves (kasoori methi),
  stalks removed
150 ml (¼ pint) warm water
2.5 ml (½ tsp) Balti Garam Masala (see page 10)
15 ml (1 tbsp) chopped fresh coriander leaves

1. Bring 350 ml (12 fl oz) water to the boil in a saucepan and add the beans. Cover the pan and bring the water back to the boil. Add the potatoes and bring back to the boil; cover and boil for 8-9 minutes, or until the vegetables are tender but the beans still have a little bite. Tip the vegetables and the cooking water into a large tray or dish to prevent the vegetables from cooking any further.
2. Preheat a karahi (Balti pan) over a medium heat and add the oil. When it is hot, but not smoking, add the fennel and cassia or cinnamon. Stir-fry for 15 seconds, then add the sliced onion, ginger and garlic. Stir-fry for 5-6 minutes, until the onion is soft and beginning to colour slightly.
3. Reduce the heat to low and add the ground coriander, cumin, turmeric and chilli powder. Stir-fry for 30 seconds and add the tomatoes. Increase the heat to medium and then stir-fry until the tomato juice has evaporated and the oil begins to float.
4. Add the cooked vegetables and cooking water, salt, fenugreek leaves and the warm water. Bring to the boil and sprinkle with the garam masala. Add the coriander leaves and stir-fry for 2-3 minutes. Remove from the heat and serve.

Preparation time: 15-20 minutes
Cooking time: 25 minutes

Dum Aloo Kashmiri

(Slow-cooked Potatoes)
Serves 4

'Dum' is a cooking method similar to pot roasting. The food is cooked in a tightly closed pot, with little or no water. This delicious potato dish from Kashmir has been adapted for cooking in a karahi (Balti pan). You will need a lid to fit your karahi, but if you do not have one, use a piece of foil. The potatoes are cooked with natural yogurt which is traditionally made of whole milk and has a rather mild taste. If you use low fat yogurt it will give a sharp flavour, which may need toning down with a little sugar.

700 g (1½ lb) small even-sized new potatoes
50 g (2 oz) ghee
two 5 cm (2 inch) pieces cassia bark or cinnamon stick
6 green cardamom pods
6 cloves
5 ml (1 tsp) fennel seeds
15 ml (1 tbsp) Ginger Paste (see page 12)
5 ml (1 tsp) ground fennel

2.5 ml (½ tsp) ground turmeric
125 g (4 oz) thick set natural yogurt, beaten until smooth
15 ml (1 tbsp) tomato purée
2.5-5 ml (½-1 tsp) chilli powder
5 ml (1 tsp) salt, or to taste
225 ml (8 fl oz) warm water
45 ml (3 tbsp) chopped fresh coriander leaves

1. Scrub and wash the potatoes well. Slice each potato crossways without cutting right through, making four to six slits on each one to allow the flavours to penetrate.
2. Preheat a karahi (Balti pan) over a medium heat for a few seconds and add the ghee. When the ghee is hot and smoke rises, fry the potatoes in batches for 8-10 minutes, until they are well browned. Remove them with a slotted spoon and drain on absorbent kitchen paper.
3. Remove the karahi from the heat, allow to cool for a few seconds, then add the cassia or cinnamon, cardamom, cloves and fennel seeds. Return the karahi to the heat and let the spices sizzle for 15 seconds.
4. Add the ginger paste and stir-fry for 1 minute, then add the ground fennel and turmeric. Stir-fry for 30 seconds and add the yogurt, tomato purée, chilli powder and salt. Mix well and add the potatoes and water. Bring to a slow simmer, cover the karahi and cook over a low heat for 25-30 minutes, until the potatoes are tender. The sauce should be rather like a thick paste at the end of the cooking time.
5. Stir in the coriander leaves and serve at once.

Preparation time: 10-15 minutes
Cooking time: 40-45 minutes

Serve with Balti Naan (see page 108) and Do-Piaza Murgh, Rogan Josh or Murgh Korma Shahi (see page 36, 18 or 38).

Not suitable for freezing.

Aloo-Brinjal

(Potatoes with Aubergine)
Serves 4

There are different varieties of aubergines available in the market these days. The most common are the long, purple ones, which are ideal for this recipe. Aubergines are rich in vitamin C and dietary fibre: cooked with potatoes as in the recipe below, they make a delicious dish. I use boiled potatoes for this recipe; you can boil the potatoes ahead and safely leave them in the refrigerator for a couple of days.

1 large, purple aubergine, about 350 g (12 oz)

salt

225 g (8 oz) old potatoes, boiled in their skins, cooled and peeled

45 ml (3 tbsp) sunflower, corn or vegetable oil

2.5 ml (½ tsp) black mustard seeds

2.5 ml (½ tsp) onion seeds (kalonji)

1 medium onion, finely chopped

10 ml (2 tsp) Ginger Paste (see page 12)

10 ml (2 tsp) Garlic Paste (see page 12)

5 ml (1 tsp) ground fennel

10 ml (2 tsp) ground cumin

5 ml (2 tsp) ground turmeric

22.5-5 ml (½-1 tsp) chilli powder

5 ml (1 tsp) salt, or to taste

450 ml (15 fl oz) warm water

40 g (1½ oz) tomato purée

5 ml (1 tsp) Balti Garam Masala (see page 10)

45 ml (3 tbsp) chopped fresh coriander

1. Quarter the aubergine lengthways and cut the stem end of each quarter into 5 cm (2 inch) pieces. Halve the remaining part of the quarters lengthways and cut into 5 cm (2 inch) pieces. Soak the aubergine in a large bowl of water with 2 teaspoons salt for 30 minutes. Drain and rinse.

2. Cut the potatoes into 5 cm (2 inch) cubes.

3. Preheat a karahi (Balti pan) or wok over a medium heat for a few seconds and add the oil. When hot but not smoking, add the mustard seeds. As soon as they pop, add the onion seeds and then the onion. Stir-fry for 6-8 minutes, or until the onion begins to colour.

4. Add the ginger and garlic and stir-fry for 1 minute, then add the ground fennel and cumin and stir-fry for 30 seconds. Add the turmeric and chilli powder, and stir-fry for 15-20 seconds. Add the salt, warm water, aubergine and tomato purée. Bring to the boil, then reduce the heat to medium and cook, uncovered, for 10 minutes, stirring frequently to ensure the aubergine cooks evenly. At the start of cooking, the aubergine will float, but once it soaks up the liquid it will sink and cook quite fast. When the aubergine sinks, add the potatoes and cook for 2-3 minutes, stirring and re-positioning the vegetables.

5. Sprinkle the garam masala over the vegetables, stir in the coriander and serve.

Preparation time: 20 minutes, plus soaking time
Cooking time: 30-35 minutes

Serve with Masala Roti and Kadhai Murgh (see pages 113 and 42); or Kheema Naan and Reshmi Kabab (see pages 109 and 65).

Not suitable for freezing.

Aloo-Brinjal

Baigan Bharta

(Spiced Puréed Aubergine)
Serves 4-6

This classic dish from the state of Punjab is traditionally made by cooking the aubergine over charcoal or burnt down ashes of a wood fire, so it is excellent cooked on a barbecue. For this recipe, I have cooked the aubergine under a hot grill.

1 large aubergine, about 350 g (12 oz)
45 ml (3 tbsp) sunflower or corn oil
10 ml (2 tsp) Ginger Paste (see page 12)
5 ml (1 tsp) Garlic Paste (see page 12)
1 fresh green chilli, seeded and cut into julienne strips
1 large onion, finely chopped
15 ml (1 tbsp) dhanna-jeera powder
2.5 ml (½ tsp) ground turmeric
1.25-2.5 ml (¼-½ tsp) chilli powder

15 ml (1 tbsp) dried fenugreek leaves (kasoori methi), stalks removed and pounded
200 g (7 oz) canned chopped tomatoes including the juice
5 ml (1 tsp) salt, or to taste
2.5 ml (½ tsp) Balti Garam Masala (see page 10)
150 ml (¼ pint) warm water
30 ml (2 tbsp) chopped fresh coriander leaves

1. Preheat the grill to medium.

2. Make three or four slits lengthways on the aubergine without cutting right through. This is to prevent it bursting during cooking. Place the aubergine in the grill pan and cook it about 10 cm (4 inches) below the element for 15-20 minutes, or until it shrinks slightly and feels soft to the touch, turning the aubergine over halfway through the cooking time. Remove and allow to cool completely.

3. Halve the aubergine lengthways and scrape the flesh with a spoon or knife. Place it in a mixing bowl or on a large plate and mash with a fork or potato masher, or purée it in a food processor.

4. Preheat a karahi (Balti pan) over a medium heat for 1-2 minutes and add the oil. When hot, but not smoking, add the ginger, garlic and fresh chilli. Stir-fry for 30 seconds.

5. Add the onion and increase the heat slightly. Stir-fry for 3-4 minutes, or until the onion begins to colour. Add the dhanna-jeera powder and turmeric, stir-fry for 1 minute, then add the chilli powder, fenugreek leaves and tomatoes. Stir-fry for 2 minutes.

6. Add the puréed or mashed aubergine, salt and garam masala and stir-fry for 2 minutes.

7. Pour in the warm water and cook for 2 minutes. Add the coriander leaves, stir and cook for 30 seconds. Serve at once.

Preparation time: 20-25 minutes, including grilling the aubergine
Cooking time: 12-15 minutes

Serve with Kheema Naan (see page 109), or as an accompaniment to Do-Piaza Murgh, Dahi ka Kheema or Aloo Gosht (see page 36, 30 or 15). Can also be served with a dhal and bread or rice of your choice for a vegetarian meal.

Imliwali Simla Mirchi

(Peppers in Tamarind Juice)
Serves 4-6

Beautiful red and green peppers are grown extensively in the hilly terrain of Northern India. In this recipe I have also included the lovely sweet yellow pepper which is available in most supermarkets.

1 sweet red pepper, about 150 g (5 oz)
1 green pepper, about 150 g (5 oz)
1 sweet yellow pepper, about 150 g (5 oz)
200 g (7 oz) potatoes, peeled and cut into 2.5 cm (1 inch) cubes
30 ml (2 tbsp) sesame seeds
15 ml (1 tbsp) white poppy seeds
10 ml (2 tsp) channa dhal or yellow split peas
8 black peppercorns
1 long, slim dried red chilli, chopped

45 ml (3 tbsp) sunflower or corn oil
2.5 ml (½ tsp) black mustard seeds
1.25 ml (¼ tsp) fenugreek seeds
1.25 ml (¼ tsp) ground turmeric
50 g (2 oz) raw cashew nuts, split
5 ml (1 tsp) salt, or to taste
2.5 ml (½ tsp) tamarind concentrate or 22.5 ml (1½ tbsp) lime juice
150 ml (¼ pint) boiling water
20 ml (4 tsp) soft brown sugar

1. Remove the core and seeds from the peppers and cut them into 2.5 cm (1 inch) cubes.

2. Bring 300 ml (½ pint) water to the boil in a karahi (Balti pan) or saucepan and add the potatoes. Bring back to the boil, cover with a lid or piece of foil and cook for 5 minutes, or until the potatoes are tender. Remove them with a slotted spoon and spread on a plate to prevent further cooking. Reserve the cooking liquid.

3. In a coffee grinder, finely grind the sesame and poppy seeds, channa dhal or yellow split peas, peppercorns and dried chilli.

4. Preheat the karahi over a medium heat for a few seconds and add the oil. When hot, but not smoking, add the mustard seeds. As soon as they pop, add the fenugreek seeds and immediately follow with the ground ingredients, turmeric and cashew nuts. Increase the heat slightly and stir-fry for 30 seconds.

5. Add the peppers and salt and stir-fry for 1 minute, then add the potatoes and reserved liquid. Stir and cook for 1 minute.

6. Blend the tamarind with the boiling water and add to the vegetables. Do not worry if the tamarind is not fully dissolved when you add it; it will soon dissolve in the karahi.

7. Add the sugar and reduce the heat to medium; cook for 5-6 minutes stirring frequently. Remove from the heat and serve at once.

Preparation time: 25 minutes
Cooking time: 10-12 minutes

Serve as an accompaniment to Kadhai Gosht Do-Piaza, Hirran Ka Gosht Masala or Kadhai Murgh
(see page 24, 25 or 42).

Suitable for freezing without the potatoes; add the boiled and diced potatoes during reheating.

Overleaf: Imliwali Simla Mirchi (left) and Methi Chaman (right)

Methi Chaman

(Indian Cheese with Fenugreek and Spinach)
Serves 4

Fenugreek is an essential flavouring in Balti cooking and is used in many recipes. Paneer is an Indian cheese which contains the same amount of protein as meat, making it ideal for a vegetarian diet. It is sold in Indian shops and some supermarkets, but it is easy to make at home (see recipe, page 13). Traditionally, puréed spinach is used for this recipe. If I am in a hurry, I use frozen, finely chopped cubes of spinach which are almost like a purée. However, I prefer the chunkiness of freshly chopped spinach.

225 g (8 oz) paneer
225 g (8 oz) fresh spinach
1 large onion, roughly chopped
25 g (1 oz) fresh root ginger, peeled and roughly
  chopped
4 large or 6 small garlic cloves, peeled and roughly
  chopped
15 ml (1 tbsp) dried fenugreek leaves (kasoori methi)
  stalks removed
50 g (2 oz) ghee or unsalted butter

10 ml (2 tsp) dhanna-jeera powder
5 ml (1 tsp) ground turmeric
2.5 ml (½ tsp) chilli powder, or to taste
2 fresh tomatoes, skinned and chopped, or 150 g
  (5 oz) chopped canned tomatoes with the juice
5 ml (1 tsp) salt, or to taste
175 ml (6 fl oz) warm water
15 ml (1 tbsp) tomato purée
2.5 ml (½ tsp) Balti Garam Masala (see page 10)

1. Cut the paneer into 2.5 cm (1 inch) cubes. Wash the spinach thoroughly and chop finely.

2. In a blender or food processor, purée the chopped onion, ginger, garlic and fenugreek leaves with 30-45 ml (2-3 tbsp) water and set aside.

3. Melt the ghee or butter in a karahi (Balti pan) over a medium heat. When hot, but not smoking, brown the cubes of paneer, taking care as it tends to splatter when the fat gets hot. Drain on absorbent kitchen paper.

4. In the ghee remaining in the karahi, stir-fry the puréed ingredients for 5-6 minutes, or until the fat becomes visible again. Add the dhanna-jeera powder and stir-fry for 30 seconds, then add the spinach. Stir-fry until all the juices have evaporated, scraping and mixing anything that sticks to the bottom of the pan. This adds extra flavour as long as you do not allow it to burn.

5. Add the turmeric and chilli powder and stir-fry for 30 seconds. Add the tomatoes and salt and stir-fry for 2-3 minutes, scraping and mixing as necessary.

6. Add the water and tomato purée and bring to the boil; reduce the heat to low, cover the karahi with a lid or piece of foil and simmer for 5 minutes.

7. Add the paneer, re-cover and simmer for 6-8 minutes. Sprinkle with the garam masala and stir-fry for 1 minute. Remove from the heat and serve.

Variation: Use tofu instead of paneer.

Preparation time: 25-30 minutes
Cooking time: 30-35 minutes

Serve with Balti Naan (see page 108). It can also be accompanied by Rogan Josh or Do-Piaza Murgh (see page 18 or 36).

Suitable for freezing.

Kadhai Paneer-Choley

(Indian Cheese and Chick Peas)
Serves 4

Paneer, the Indian cheese, is a very versatile and popular ingredient. In a country renowned for its vegetarian cuisine, paneer is very important as a source of protein and essential nutrients. Tofu, which is available from larger supermarkets and health food shops, is a good alternative.

40 g (1½ oz) ghee or unsalted butter
5 ml (1 tsp) Ginger Paste (see page 12)
5 ml (1 tsp) Garlic Paste (see page 12)
5 ml (1 tsp) dhanna-jeera powder
2.5 ml (½ tsp) ground turmeric
1.25 ml (¼ tsp) chilli powder
400 g (14 oz) can chick peas, drained and rinsed
150 ml (¼ pint) warm water
450 ml (15 fl oz) Kadhai Gravy (see page 12)

2.5 ml (½ tsp) salt, or to taste
225 g (8 oz) Paneer (see page 13), cut into 2.5 cm (1 inch) cubes
10 ml (2 tsp) dried fenugreek leaves (kasoori methi), stalks removed
100 g (4 oz) green pepper, cored, seeded and cut into julienne strips
30 ml (2 tbsp) chopped fresh coriander leaves

1. Preheat a karahi (Balti pan) over a medium heat for a few seconds and add the ghee or butter. When hot, stir-fry the ginger and garlic for 30 seconds.
2. Add the dhanna-jeera powder, turmeric and chilli powder. Stir-fry for 1 minute, then add the chick peas and stir-fry for 2 minutes. Pour in the warm water, bring to the boil and allow to boil steadily for 2 minutes.
3. Add the kadhai gravy, salt and paneer. Bring to the boil, then simmer, uncovered, for 6-7 minutes.
4. Add the fenugreek leaves and pepper strips. Simmer for 2-3 minutes. Stir in the coriander leaves, remove from the heat and serve.

Variation: Use prawns instead of paneer.

Preparation time: 10 minutes, plus cooking the Kadhai Gravy
Cooking time: 15 minutes

Serve accompanied by Kadhai Murgh, Turkey Narangi or Kadhai Gosht Do-Piaza (see page 42, 37 or 24). Makes a balanced vegetarian meal with naan or rice and a raita

Suitable for freezing.

→***Cook's tip:*** Make a delicious instant pulao with the leftovers by mixing it with Tala hua Chawal (see page 103) and serve with any vegetable curry.

Sabzi Masala Malai

(Vegetables in a Spicy Cream Sauce)
Serves 4-6

Sabzi refers to vegetables and masala means a blend of spices. Malai is cream which can be either dairy cream or one that is extracted from fresh coconut.

200 g (7 oz) fresh thin green beans, trimmed and cut into pieces

200 g (7 oz) baby carrots, peeled and left whole or cut into pieces

200 g (7 oz) old potatoes, not floury ones, peeled and cut into 2.5 cm (1 inch) cubes

25 g (1 oz) ghee or unsalted butter

5 ml (1 tsp) shahi jeera (royal cumin)

4 green cardamom pods, the top of each pod split to release the flavour

1 medium onion, finely chopped

6 garlic cloves, peeled and crushed

2.5 cm (1 inch) piece fresh root ginger, peeled and finely grated

15 ml (1 tbsp) dhanna-jeera powder

2.5 ml (½ tsp) ground turmeric

2.5 ml (½ tsp) chilli powder

5 ml (1 tsp) Balti Garam Masala (see page 10)

150 g (5 oz) canned chopped tomatoes including the juice

5 ml (1 tsp) salt, or to taste

2.5 ml (½ tsp) dried mint

150 ml (¼ pint) warm water

75 ml (3 fl oz) single cream

1. Put 450 ml (15 fl oz) water into a karahi (Balti pan) or saucepan and bring to the boil. Add the beans, bring back to boil and cook for 2 minutes. Add the carrots and potatoes and bring back to the boil. Cover the pan with a lid or a piece of foil and simmer for 5 minutes. Remove the vegetables with a slotted spoon and spread out on a large plate to prevent further cooking. Reserve the cooking liquid.

2. Preheat the karahi over a medium heat for a few seconds and add the ghee or butter. As soon as the fat melts, add the shahi jeera and cardamom and fry for 15 seconds.

3. Add the onion, garlic and ginger and stir fry for 3-4 minutes, or until the onion is soft. Reduce the heat to low and add the dhanna-jeera powder, turmeric, chilli powder and half the garam masala. Stir-fry for 1 minute.

4. Add the tomatoes, increase the heat to medium and stir-fry for 2 minutes. Add the cooked vegetables, reserved liquid, salt, mint and warm water. Bring to the boil and simmer for 2-3 minutes, uncovered.

5. Pour in the cream, sprinkle with the remaining garam masala and simmer for 2 minutes. Serve at once.

Preparation time: 25 minutes
Cooking time: 20 minutes

Serve accompanied by Murgh Korma Shahi, Rogan Josh or Rista (see page 38, 18 or 28).

→**Cook's tip:** If you have any leftovers, mix it with freshly cooked basmati rice to make an excellent vegetable pulao. Mix half the quantity of vegetables to rice. If you have leftover plain boiled rice, reheat the rice and vegetables separately, then mix together gently with a fork.

Sabzi Masala Malai

Lobia Khumb

(Black-eyed Beans with Mushrooms)
Serves 4

Black-eyed beans are available in most supermarkets and health food shops. I have used canned beans but you can use dried beans which you will need to soak and cook first.

1 onion, roughly chopped
4-5 garlic cloves, peeled and roughly chopped
2.5 cm (1 inch) piece fresh root ginger, peeled and roughly chopped
60 ml (4 tbsp) sunflower or corn oil
5 ml (1 tsp) shahi jeera (royal cumin)
two 2.5 cm (1 inch) pieces cassia bark or cinnamon sticks
10 ml (2 tsp) ground cumin
5 ml (1 tsp) ground coriander
2.5 ml (½ tsp) ground fennel
5 ml (1 tsp) ground turmeric

1.25-2.5 ml (¼-½ tsp) chilli powder
175 g (6 oz) canned chopped tomatoes including the juice
100 g (4 oz) large flat mushrooms, wiped and cut into bite-sized pieces
225 ml (8 fl oz) warm water
5 ml (1 tsp) dried mint
410 g (14 oz) can black-eyed beans, drained and rinsed
2.5 ml (½ tsp) salt, or to taste
1.25 ml (¼ tsp) Balti Garam Masala (see page 10)
30 ml (2 tbsp) chopped fresh coriander leaves

1. In a blender or food processor, purée the onion, garlic and ginger, adding a little water if necessary. Set aside.

2. Preheat a karahi (Balti pan) over a medium heat and add the oil. When hot, but not smoking, add the shahi jeera and cassia or cinnamon. Stir-fry for 15-20 seconds. Add the cumin, coriander and fennel and stir-fry for a further 30 seconds. Add the puréed ingredients. Stir-fry for 4-5 minutes, reducing the heat slightly halfway through.

3. Add the turmeric and chilli powder; stir-fry for 1 minute and add half the tomatoes. Stir-fry for 2-3 minutes or until oil surfaces on the spice paste.

4. Add the mushrooms, warm water and mint, bring to the boil, cover with a lid or a piece of foil and simmer for 5 minutes.

5. Add the beans, salt and remaining tomatoes and simmer, uncovered, for 5 minutes. Stir in the garam masala and coriander leaves. Remove from the heat and serve.

Preparation time: 15-20 minutes
Cooking time: 20 minutes

Serve with Kheema Naan (see page 109) or accompanied by any kabab, Tandoori Murgh (see page 68) or Machchi Badami (see page 53).

Suitable for freezing.

→***Cook's tip:*** Mix with plain boiled basmati rice to make an instant pulao. Garnish with sliced, hard-boiled eggs. Serve with any raita and pappadum.

Kadhai Dhal Makhani

(Balti Dhal with Butter)
Serves 4

Dhal Makhani is one of the best known and loved lentil delicacies in India. Traditionally, whole masoor dhal (whole red lentils) are used, which you can buy from Indian grocers, but in this recipe I have used yellow split peas as they are widely available. They are similar in appearance to channa dhal which are also excellent for this recipe.

175 g (6 oz) yellow split peas, washed and soaked for
   3-4 hours, then drained
5 ml (1 tsp) salt, or to taste
5 ml (1 tsp) ground turmeric
15 ml (1 tbsp) Garlic Paste (see page 12)
15 ml (1 tbsp) Ginger Paste (see page 12)
1-2 fresh green chillies, seeded and sliced lengthways
25 g (1 oz) tomato purée

150 g (5 oz) fresh tomatoes, peeled and
   chopped, or canned chopped tomatoes with the juice
50 g (2 oz) butter
200 ml (7 fl oz) single cream
15 ml (1 tbsp) chopped fresh mint leaves or 5 ml
   (1 tsp) dried mint
15 g (½ oz) chopped fresh coriander leaves

1. Put the peas, salt, turmeric, garlic and ginger in a karahi (Balti pan) with 600 ml (1 pint) water and bring to the boil. Reduce the heat to low, cover the karahi with a lid or a piece of foil and simmer for 25-30 minutes, stirring halfway through.
2. Mash some of the peas with the back of the spoon to thicken the dhal. Add the chillies, tomato purée, tomatoes, butter, cream and mint. Cook gently for 5 minutes, uncovered. Stir in the coriander leaves and serve.

Preparation time: 5-10 minutes, plus soaking time
Cooking time: 30-35 minutes

Serve with any bread, accompanied by kababs, Tandoori Murgh or Machchi Badami
(see page 68 or 53).

Suitable for freezing.

Amritsari Dhal

(Amritsar-style Dhal)
Serves 4

The state of Punjab gets its name from 'Punj' meaning five and 'ab' meaning rivers. It is well known for its excellent repertoire of recipes. This recipe comes from Amritsar, a city in the Punjab, almost bordering on to Pakistan, and also close to Kashmir.

75 g (3 oz) masoor dhal (red split lentils)
75 g (3 oz) channa dhal or yellow split lentils
45 ml (3 tbsp) sunflower or corn oil
5 ml (1 tsp) shahi jeera (royal cumin)
2.5 cm (1 inch) piece fresh root ginger, peeled and finely grated
6 garlic cloves, peeled and crushed
8-10 curry leaves (optional)
1 large onion, finely chopped

1 fresh green chilli, seeded and finely chopped
1 long slim dried red chilli, chopped
5 ml (1 tsp) ground turmeric
5 ml (1 tsp) salt, or to taste
600 ml (1 pint) warm water
5 ml (1 tsp) dried mint
40 g (1½ oz) butter
30 ml (2 tbsp) finely chopped fresh coriander leaves

1. Pick over, wash and soak the lentils in cold water for 1-2 hours, then drain.
2. Preheat a karahi or wok over a medium heat and add the oil. When hot, but not smoking, add the shahi jeera and fry for 15 seconds.
3. Add the ginger, garlic and curry leaves, if using, and stir-fry for 30 seconds. Add the onion and stir-fry for 5-6 minutes, or until the onion begins to colour.
4. Add the fresh and dried chillies, turmeric, lentils and salt. Stir-fry for 5-6 minutes, reducing the heat slightly halfway through.
5. Pour in the warm water, bring to the boil and cook for 2 minutes. Reduce the heat to low and cover the karahi with a lid or a piece of foil. Simmer for 25 minutes.
6. Stir in the mint, re-cover and simmer for a further 5-6 minutes.
7. Add the butter and fresh coriander. Stir and cook until the butter has melted, then serve at once.

Preparation time: 25 minutes, plus soaking time
Cooking time: 50-55 minutes

Serve with Kheema Naan (see page 109), Masala Roti (see page 113) or plain boiled basmati rice, accompanied by any kebab or Hara Masala ki Machchi (see page 61).

Suitable for freezing.

Kadhai Dhal Makhani (left) and Amritsari Dhal (right)

RESTAURANT-STYLE DISHES

Balti combination dishes are quick and simple to prepare, fun to cook and make excellent balanced meals. Almost every Balti restaurant I have visited in Birmingham has an amazing selection of combination dishes. To the Baltistanis it made perfect sense to combine meat, lentils and vegetables in one dish to save valuable cooking fuel. Using just one pot to cook everything, then eating straight out of it was also perfect for a nomadic life-style. In this chapter, I have created a few simple combination recipes which you can cook from scratch or use leftovers to create exciting new dishes.

Gosht-Saag-Channa

(Lamb with Spinach and Chick Peas)
Serves 4-6

This combination looks attractive and the chick peas add a lovely, nutty flavour. I have used canned chick peas which only need to be drained and rinsed before use, but you can use dried chick peas – they will need soaking overnight and boiling until tender.

30 ml (2 tbsp) sunflower, corn or vegetable oil
5 ml (1 tsp) Ginger Paste (see page 12)
5 ml (1 tsp) Garlic Paste (see page 12)
5 cm (2 inch) piece cassia bark or cinnamon stick, halved
5 ml (1 tsp) ground cumin
5 ml (1 tsp) ground coriander
1.25 ml (¼ tsp) ground turmeric
2.5 ml (½ tsp) chilli powder, or to taste
400 g (14 oz) can of chick peas, drained and rinsed thoroughly

450 g (1 lb) pre-cooked lamb (see page 14)
5 ml (1 tsp) salt, or to taste
450 ml (15 fl oz) Kadhai Gravy (see page 12)
450 ml (15 fl oz) reserved stock or stock and water
225 g (8 oz) fresh spinach, chopped, or frozen leaf spinach, thawed and drained
2.5 ml (½ tsp) Balti Garam Masala (see page 10)
30 ml (2 tbsp) chopped fresh coriander leaves

1. Preheat a karahi (Balti pan) over a medium heat and add the oil. When hot, add the ginger, garlic and cassia or cinnamon and stir-fry for 30 seconds.
2. Add the cumin, coriander, turmeric and chilli powder, stir-fry for 30 seconds and add the chick peas, cooked lamb and salt. Stir-fry for 2-3 minutes, then add the gravy. Bring to the boil over a high heat and add the stock, or stock and water. Bring to the boil again and reduce the heat to medium. Cook, uncovered, for 10-15 minutes, or until the sauce has thickened, stirring occasionally.
3. Add the spinach and cook for 5-6 minutes. Stir in the garam masala and coriander leaves and serve.

Preparation time: 15 minutes, plus time for pre-cooking the lamb and Kadhai Gravy
Cooking time: 25 minutes

Serve with any bread or Tala hua Chawal (see page 103) and a raita, if liked.

Suitable for freezing if fresh spinach is used.

Gosht-Gobi-Aloo-Mirchi

(Lamb with Cabbage, Potatoes and Peppers)
Serves 4-6

This is a colourful dish with a lovely fresh aroma. Make sure that the cabbage and peppers are not overcooked, they should be tender but still have plenty of bite.

30 ml (2 tbsp) sunflower, corn or vegetable oil
2.5 ml (½ tsp) Ginger Paste (see page 12)
2.5 ml (½ tsp) Garlic Paste (see page 12)
1 small onion, finely chopped
2.5 ml (½ tsp) ground cumin
5 ml (1 tsp) ground coriander
1.25 ml (¼ tsp) ground turmeric
2.5 ml (½ tsp) chilli powder, or to taste
450 g (1 lb) pre-cooked lamb (see page 14)
5 ml (1 tsp) salt, or to taste

450 ml (15 fl oz) Kadhai Gravy (see page 12)
300 g (10 oz) white cabbage, coarsely chopped
300 ml (½ pint) reserved stock or stock and water
300 g (10 oz) pre-boiled potatoes, peeled and cut into 5 cm (2 inch) cubes
75 g (3 oz) sweet red pepper, cut into 5 cm (2 inch) cubes
2.5 ml (½ tsp) dried mint
2.5 ml (½ tsp) Balti Garam Masala
30 ml (2 tbsp) chopped fresh coriander leaves

1. Preheat a karahi (Balti pan) over a medium heat and add the oil. When hot, add the ginger and garlic and stir-fry for 15 seconds. Add the onion and stir-fry for 5-6 minutes, until the onion begins to colour.

2. Add the ground cumin, coriander, turmeric and chilli powder. Stir-fry for 30 seconds. Add the cooked lamb and salt and stir-fry for 2-3 minutes. Add the gravy, bring to the boil over a high heat, then reduce the heat to medium and cook, uncovered, for 10 minutes, stirring occasionally.

3. Add the cabbage and reserved stock, or stock and water. Bring to the boil again and reduce the heat to medium. Cover the karahi with a lid or piece of foil and cook for 7-10 minutes, or until the cabbage is tender but still firm.

4. Add the potatoes and pepper and cook, uncovered, for 5 minutes. Stir in the mint, garam masala and chopped coriander. Serve at once.

Variation: Use cauliflower instead of cabbage. Cook cauliflower for 5 minutes before adding the potatoes and peppers.

Preparation time: 20-25 minutes, plus time for pre-cooking the lamb and Kadhai Gravy
Cooking time: 35 minutes

Serve with Balti Naan or Sheermal (see page 108 or 110).

Suitable for freezing, but freeze at the end of step 3. Thaw and complete step 4.

Gosht-Dhal-Ghia-Mirchi

(Lamb with Lentils, Marrow and Peppers)
Serves 4-6

Although this dish is a combination of four main ingredients, it is quick to put together if the lamb and the channa dhal are pre-cooked. As well as keeping cooked lamb in your freezer, it is a good idea to freeze a quantity of lentils too. Marrow is traditional and can be be used when in season. I have used courgettes instead.

100 g (4 oz) channa dhal or yellow split peas
45 ml (3 tbsp) sunflower, corn or vegetable oil
5 ml (1 tsp) fennel seeds
2.5 ml (½ tsp) crushed dried chillies
1 medium onion, finely sliced
450 g (1 lb) pre-cooked lamb (see page 14)
5 ml (1 tsp) Ginger Paste (see page 12)
5 ml (1 tsp) Garlic Paste (see page 12)
7.5 ml (1½ tsp) dhanna-jeera powder
7.5 ml (1½ tsp) ground turmeric

2.5 ml (½ tsp) chilli powder, or to taste
300 ml (½ pint) reserved stock or stock and water
450 ml (15 fl oz) Kadhai Gravy (see page 12)
5 ml (1 tsp) salt, or to taste
225 g (8 oz) courgettes, quartered lengthways and cut into 2.5 cm (1 inch) pieces
2.5 ml (½ tsp) dried mint
1 small sweet red pepper, cut into 5 cm (2 inch) pieces
2.5 ml (½ tsp) Balti Garam Masala (see page 10)
45 ml (3 tbsp) chopped fresh coriander leaves

1. Clean and pick over the channa dhal and soak them in plenty of cold water for 1-2 hours. Drain and put them into a saucepan with 475 ml (16 fl oz) water. Place over a high heat and bring to the boil, reduce the heat to medium and cook, uncovered for 6-7 minutes. Cover the pan with a lid or piece of foil, reduce the heat to low and simmer for 12-13 minutes, or until the dhal absorbs all the water. Remove the lid and boil to evaporate the excess liquid, if necessary. The grains should be tender, but not mushy. Remove from the heat and set aside.

2. Preheat a karahi (Balti pan) over a medium heat and add the oil. When hot, but not smoking, add the fennel and crushed chillies and let them sizzle for 15 seconds. Add the onion and stir-fry for 6-7 minutes, until it begins to colour.

3. Add the cooked meat, ginger, garlic, dhanna-jeera powder, turmeric and chilli powder. Stir-fry for 1 minute and add half the reserved stock, or stock and water. Increase the heat to high and cook for 4-5 minutes, or until the liquid evaporates and the oil begins to separate from the rest of the ingredients, stirring frequently.

4. Add the gravy and bring to the boil. Reduce the heat to medium and cook for 3-4 minutes, stirring frequently. Add the remaining stock, salt, courgettes, mint and the cooked dhal. Bring back to the boil and cook over a medium heat for 3-4 minutes, stirring frequently.

5. Add the pepper, garam masala and coriander leaves. Increase the heat to high and stir-fry for 1-2 minutes. Remove from the heat and serve.

Preparation time: 20 minutes, plus soaking time for the dhal and pre-cooking time for the lamb and Kadhai Gravy
Cooking time: 40 minutes

Serve with plain boiled basmati rice or any bread and a raita or chutney.

Suitable for freezing.

Gosht-Ghia-Dhal-Mirchi with Pudina-Dhaniya ki Chutney

Gosht-Aloo-Saag

(Lamb with Potato and Spinach)
Serves 4-6

Lamb with spinach is a classic combination and one of the delicacies of the north. Adding potatoes makes the recipe more interesting and also makes it go further!

30 ml (2 tbsp) sunflower, corn or vegetable oil
5 ml (1 tsp) Ginger Paste (see page 12)
5 ml (1 tsp) Garlic Paste (see page 12)
5 ml (1 tsp) dhanna-jeera powder
2.5 ml (½ tsp) chilli powder or to taste
1.25 ml (¼ tsp) ground turmeric
450 g (1 lb) pre-cooked lamb (see page 14)
5 ml (1 tsp) salt, or to taste

450 ml (15 fl oz) Karahi Gravy (see page 12)
450 g (1 lb) reserved stock or stock and water
300 g (10 oz) pre-boiled potatoes, peeled and
cut into 5 cm (2 inch) cubes
225 g (8 oz) fresh spinach, chopped, or frozen
leaf spinach, thawed and drained
2.5 ml (½ tsp) Balti Garam Masala(see page 10)
30 ml (2 tbsp) chopped fresh coriander leaves

1. Preheat a karahi (Balti pan) over a medium heat and add the oil. When hot, add the ginger and garlic and stir-fry for 30 seconds. Add the dhanna-jeera powder, chilli powder and turmeric and stir-fry for 30 seconds.
2. Add the cooked lamb and salt and stir-fry for 3-4 minutes, scraping and mixing any spices that stick to the bottom and sides of the karahi.
3. Stir in the gravy, bring to the boil over a high heat, then add the stock or stock and water. Bring to the boil again, reduce the heat to medium and cook, uncovered, for 10-15 minutes.
4. Add the potatoes and the spinach and continue to cook for a further 5-7 minutes, or until the sauce has thickened. Sprinkle in the garam masala and chopped coriander, stir and cook for 1 minute before serving.

Preparation time: 15 minutes, plus cooking time for the Karahi Gravy
Cooking time: 25-30 minutes

Serve with Balti Naan or Pudina Pyaz ki Roti (see page 108 or 112).

Not suitable for freezing.

→*Cook's tip:* If you have leftover Aloo Gosht (see page 15), weigh it and add half its weight of fresh or frozen spinach. Stir-fry everything together with a little water, if necessary. Adjust salt and garam masala and garnish with fresh coriander.

Kheema-Aloo-Mattar

(Minced Lamb with Potatoes and Peas)
Serves 4

Aloo Mattar (potatoes and peas) and Kheema Mattar (mince and peas) are two popular combinations in Northern India. I have put them together to create this Birmingham-style Balti restaurant dish.

50 ml (2 fl oz) sunflower, corn or vegetable oil
225 g (8 oz) old potatoes, peeled and cut into 2.5 cm
    (1 inch) cubes
15 ml (1 tbsp) ghee or unsalted butter
2.5 ml (½ tsp) cumin seeds
2.5 ml (½ tsp) onion seeds (kalonji)
1 small onion, finely chopped
300 g (10 oz) minced lamb or beef
5 ml (1 tsp) Ginger Paste (see page 12)
5 ml (1 tsp) Garlic Paste (see page 12)

10 ml (2 tsp) dhanna-jeera powder
1.25 ml (¼ tsp) ground turmeric
1.25-2.5 ml (¼-½ tsp) chilli powder
150 ml (¼ pint) warm water
450 ml (15 fl oz) Kadhai Gravy (see page 12)
5 ml (1 tsp) salt, or to taste
2.5 ml (½ tsp) dried mint
100 g (4 oz) frozen garden peas
45 ml (3 tbsp) chopped fresh coriander leaves
2.5 ml (½ tsp) Balti Garam Masala (see page 10)

1. Preheat a karahi (Balti pan) over a medium heat and add the oil. When hot, add the potatoes and stir-fry for 5-7 minutes, until they are well-browned. It doesn't matter if the potatoes stick to the pan slightly, this can be stirred and mixed into the spices later. Drain the potatoes on absorbent kitchen paper.
2. Reduce the heat slightly and add the ghee or butter. Stir-fry the cumin and onion seeds for 15 seconds and add the onion. Increase the heat to medium and stir-fry the onion for 6-7 minutes, until beginning to colour.
3. Add the mince and increase the heat slightly. Stir-fry for 3-4 minutes and add the ginger and garlic. Continue to stir-fry for 1-2 minutes and add the dhanna-jeera powder, turmeric and chilli powder. Stir-fry for a further 1-2 minutes and add the fried potatoes and water. Bring to the boil and add the gravy, salt and mint. Stir until the contents begin to bubble, reduce the heat to low, cover the karahi with a lid or piece of foil and simmer for 15-20 minutes, or until the potatoes are tender.
4. Add the peas and simmer, uncovered, for 5 minutes. Stir in the chopped coriander leaves and garam masala and serve at once.

Preparation time: 15 minutes, plus cooking time for the Kadhai Gravy
Cooking time: 35-40 minutes

Serve with Balti Naan or Masala Roti (see page 108 or 113).

Not suitable for freezing.

Murgh-Makki-Khumb

(Chicken with Sweetcorn and Mushrooms)
Serves 4-5

I was surprised to discover that people in the West did not associate sweetcorn with Indian cooking. It is, in fact, a much used and loved vegetable. I am sure you will be delighted with this particular combination.

60 ml (4 tbsp) sunflower, corn or vegetable oil
1 medium onion, finely sliced
5 ml (1 tsp) cumin seeds
5 ml (1 tsp) Ginger Paste (see page 12)
5 ml (1 tsp) Garlic Paste (see page 12)
450 g (1 lb) boned chicken thighs or breast, skinned and cut into 5 cm (2 inch) cubes
2.5 ml (½ tsp) ground fennel
5 ml (1 tsp) ground coriander
2.5 ml (½ tsp) ground turmeric
2.5 ml (½ tsp) chilli powder, or to taste

50 g (2 oz) natural yogurt
225 g (8 oz) closed cup mushrooms, thickly sliced
300 ml (½ pint) Makhani Gravy (see page 13)
5 ml (1 tsp) salt, or to taste
175 g (6 oz) frozen sweetcorn or canned sweetcorn, drained and rinsed
2.5 ml (½ tsp) Balti Garam Masala (see page 10)
45 ml (3 tbsp) chopped fresh coriander leaves
1-4 fresh green chillies, seeded and cut into julienne strips

1. Preheat a karahi (Balti pan) over a medium heat and add the oil. When hot, add the onion slices and stir-fry for 8-9 minutes, until they are lightly browned. Remove with a slotted spoon and drain on absorbent kitchen paper.

2. Reduce the heat to low and add the cumin seeds. Let them sizzle for 15 seconds, then add the ginger and garlic. Stir-fry for 1 minute and add the chicken, fennel, coriander, turmeric and chilli powder. Increase the heat to high and stir-fry for 2 minutes, then add 75 ml (3 fl oz) water. Continue to stir-fry for 2 minutes, or until the water evaporates. Return the onion to the pan. Add another 75 ml (3 fl oz) water and stir-fry for 2 minutes. Then add the yogurt and stir-fry for 2 minutes.

3. Add the mushrooms and stir-fry for 2 minutes, then add the gravy and salt. Stir until the contents begin to bubble and reduce the heat to low. Cook, uncovered, for 5 minutes, stirring occasionally.

4. Add the sweetcorn and cook for a further 5 minutes, stirring once or twice.

5. Add the garam masala, chopped coriander and fresh chillies. Increase the heat to medium and stir-fry for 1-2 minutes. Remove from the heat and serve.

Preparation time: 25 minutes, plus cooking time for the Makhani Gravy
Cooking time: 25 minutes

Serve with Balti Naan or Masala Roti (see page 108 or 113).

Not suitable for freezing.

Murgh-Makki-Khumb

Murgh-Dhal-Mirchiwali

(Chicken with Lentils and Peppers)
Serves 4-5

This is a good example of a wholesome, balanced, all-in-one Balti dish. The base here is Makhani Gravy which complements both chicken and channa dhal extremely well. Although channa dhal and yellow split peas look similar, they vary in flavour, but the cooking time is the same for both.

100 g (4 oz) channa dhal or yellow split peas
475 ml (16 fl oz) hot water
60 ml (4 tbsp) sunflower, corn or vegetable oil
2.5 ml (½ tsp) black mustard seeds
2.5 ml (½ tsp) fennel seeds
1-2 fresh green chillies, seeded and chopped
5 ml (1 tsp) Ginger Paste (see page 12)
5 ml (1 tsp) Garlic Paste (see page 12)
1 medium onion, finely sliced
5 cm (2 inch) piece cassia bark or cinnamon stick, halved
5 ml (1 tsp) salt, or to taste
2.5 ml (½ tsp) ground turmeric

2.5 ml (½ tsp) chilli powder, or to taste
2.5 ml (½ tsp) ground fennel
5 ml (1 tsp) ground cumin
450 g (1 lb) boned chicken thighs or breasts, skinned and cut into 5 cm (2 inch) cubes
50 g (2 oz) natural yogurt
450 ml (15 fl oz) Makhani Gravy (see page 13)
2.5 ml (½ tsp) dried mint
1 small sweet red pepper, cored, seeded and cut into 2.5 cm (1 inch) dice
2.5 ml (½ tsp) Balti Garam Masala
45 ml (3 tbsp) chopped fresh coriander leaves

1. Pick over the dhal, wash and soak it in plenty of cold water for 1-2 hours. Drain well and put into a saucepan with the hot water. Bring to the boil and allow to boil steadily for 4-5 minutes. Reduce the heat to low, cover the pan and cook for 15-20 minutes, until the dhal is tender and the grains are still whole and have absorbed all the water. Remove the lid and boil to evaporate any excess liquid, if necessary. Remove from the heat and set aside.

2. Preheat a karahi (Balti pan) over a medium heat and add the oil. When hot, but not smoking, add the mustard seeds and let them pop. The oil must be fairly hot for the mustard seeds to pop and release their flavour. You can test this by putting one or two seeds in the hot oil. If they pop straight away, then the oil is at the right temperature.

3. Add the fennel seeds followed by the fresh chillies, ginger and garlic. Stir-fry for 1 minute, add the onion, cassia or cinnamon and salt and stir-fry for 5-6 minutes, until the onion has softened and is beginning to colour a little.

4. Add the turmeric, chilli powder, ground fennel and cumin. Stir-fry for 1 minute and add the chicken and yogurt. Increase the heat to high and stir-fry for a further 5-6 minutes, then add the cooked dhal and continue to stir-fry for 2-3 minutes.

5. Add the gravy and mint and stir until the contents begin to bubble. Add the pepper and cook for 2-3 minutes, then add the garam masala and coriander leaves. Stir and cook for 1-2 minutes, remove from the heat and serve.

Preparation time: 20 minutes, plus soaking time and cooking time for the Makhani Gravy
Cooking time: 40-45 minutes

Serve with Balti Naan (see page 108) or plain boiled basmati rice and a raita.

Suitable for freezing.

Murgh-Kheema-Khumb

(Chicken with Minced Lamb and Mushrooms)
Serves 4-5

This is a lovely combination, typical of the dishes served in Balti restaurants.

45 ml (3 tbsp) sunflower, corn or vegetable oil
1 medium onion, finely sliced
225 g (8 oz) minced lamb or beef
300 g (10 oz) boned chicken thighs or breast, skinned
   and cut into 5 cm (2 inch) cubes
50 g (2 oz) natural yogurt
5 ml (1 tsp) Ginger Paste (see page 12)
5 ml (1 tsp) Garlic Paste (see page 12)
5 ml (1 tsp) ground cumin
1.25 ml (¼ tsp) ground turmeric

2.5 ml (½ tsp) chilli powder, or to taste
15 ml (1 tbsp) tomato purée
5 ml (1 tsp) salt, or to taste
450 ml (15 fl oz) Kadhai Gravy (see page 12)
225 g (8 oz) closed cup mushrooms, sliced
2.5 ml (½ tsp) Balti Garam Masala (see page 10)
2.5 ml (½ tsp) dried fenugreek leaves (kasoori methi),
   stalks removed
45 ml (3 tbsp) chopped fresh coriander leaves

1. Preheat a karahi (Balti pan) over a medium heat and add the oil. When hot, add the onion and stir-fry for 6-7 minutes, until it begins to colour. Add the mince, increase the heat slightly and stir-fry the mince for 2-3 minutes, or until all the natural juices have evaporated.
2. Add the chicken and yogurt, stir-fry for 3-4 minutes, then add the ginger and garlic. Stir-fry for a further 2-3 minutes and add the cumin, turmeric and chilli powder. Continue to stir-fry for 1-2 minutes.
3. Add the tomato purée and salt, stir-fry for 1 minute and add the gravy and mushrooms. Bring to the boil, reduce the heat to low, cover the karahi with a lid or piece of foil and simmer for 10-12 minutes.
4. Add the garam masala, fenugreek leaves and chopped coriander, increase the heat to medium and stir-fry for 1-2 minutes. Remove from the heat and serve.

Variation: To create this dish instantly, just like the Balti restaurants do, mix equal quantities of cooked Do-Piaza Murgh, Kadhai Murgh or Murgh Jeera (see page 36, 42 or 48) with Kheema Do-Piaza or Dahi ka Kheema (see page 29 or 30) and add 225 g (8 oz) sliced mushrooms. Simmer gently in 150 ml (¼ pint) Kadhai Gravy (see page 12), adding a little water to dilute the sauce. Garnish with fresh coriander.

Preparation time: 15-20 minutes, plus cooking time for the Kadhai Gravy
Cooking time: 30 minutes

Serve with any bread or plain boiled basmati rice and Imliwali Simla Mirchi (see page 77) or a raita.

Suitable for freezing.

Jhinga-Palak-Paneer

(Prawns with Spinach and Indian Cheese)
Serves 4-5

Palak-Paneer is a classic dish from the state of Punjab where spinach and paneer are cooked together with herbs and spices. Paneer, which is used for both savoury and sweet dishes, easily absorbs the flavours of other ingredients. If you cannot get paneer, or do not have time to make it, you can use plain tofu which can be bought from health food stores and supermarkets.

30 ml (2 tbsp) sunflower, corn or vegetable oil
1.25 ml (¼ tsp) black mustard seeds
2.5 ml (½ tsp) fennel seeds
1 large onion, finely sliced
5 ml (1 tsp) Ginger Paste (see page 12)
5 ml (1 tsp) Garlic Paste (see page 12)
7.5 ml (1½ tsp) ground coriander
2.5 ml (½ tsp) chilli powder, or to taste
225 g (8 oz) Paneer (see page 13), cut into 2.5 cm (1 inch) cubes

225 g (8 oz) fresh spinach, chopped, or frozen leaf spinach, thawed and drained
300 ml (½ pint) Makhani Gravy (see page 13)
225 g (8 oz) shelled fresh prawns or cooked and peeled frozen prawns, thawed and drained
5 ml (1 tsp) salt, or to taste
5 ml (1 tsp) sugar
50 ml (2 fl oz) double cream
2.5 ml (½ tsp) Balti Garam Masala (see page 10)

1. Preheat a karahi (Balti pan) over a medium heat and add the oil. When hot, but not smoking, add the mustard seeds followed by the fennel. The oil must be hot enough for the mustard seeds to pop. To test this, just add one or two mustard seeds to the hot oil. If they start popping straight away then the temperature is just right.

2. Add the onion slices and stir-fry for 6-7 minutes, until they begin to colour, then add the ginger and garlic. Stir-fry for 1 minute, then add the ground coriander and chilli powder. Stir-fry for a further 1 minute, add 75 ml (3 fl oz) water and stir-fry until the water evaporates and oil floats on the surface.

3. Add the paneer and spinach and stir-fry until the spinach begins to wilt. Add the gravy. Bring to the boil, reduce the heat to low and simmer, uncovered, for 2-3 minutes.

4. Add the prawns, salt and sugar. Cook, uncovered, for 3-7 minutes depending on the type of prawns used. Add the cream and garam masala, stir-fry for 1 minute and serve.

Preparation time: 20 minutes, plus cooking time for the Makhani Gravy
Cooking time: 15-20 minutes

Serve with Sada Pulao or Balti Naan (see page 104 and 108).

Suitable for freezing if fresh prawns and fresh spinach are used.

Jhinga-Brinjal-Andey (top) and Jhinga-Palak-Paneer (bottom)

Jhinga-Brinjal-Andey

(Prawns with Aubergines and Eggs)
Serves 4-5

Aubergine is a delicious vegetable and its flavour complements prawns very well. When cooking with prawns, I prefer to peel the aubergine as the skin has a rather strong taste. Watch the aubergine carefully during cooking as the timing is very important. When you add the water, the aubergine pieces will float, but once they start absorbing the liquid, they will sink and will cook very quickly.

1 aubergine, about 300 g (10 oz)
4-5 hard-boiled eggs
45 ml (3 tbsp) sunflower, corn or vegetable oil
2.5 ml (½ tsp) onion seeds (kalonji)
1 medium onion, finely sliced
5 ml (1 tsp) Ginger Paste (see page 12)
5 ml (1 tsp) Garlic Paste (see page 12)
1-2 fresh green chillies, seeded and chopped

2.5 ml (½ tsp) ground coriander
2.5 ml (½ tsp) ground cumin
300 ml (½ pint) warm water
450 ml (15 fl oz) Makhani Gravy (see page 13)
225 g (8 oz) shelled fresh prawns or cooked and peeled frozen prawns, thawed and drained
2.5 ml (½ tsp) Balti Garam Masala (see page 10)
45 ml (3 tbsp) chopped fresh coriander leaves

1. Peel the aubergine and cut into 5 cm (2 inch) cubes. Soak it in salted water for 30 minutes, then drain and rinse.

2. Shell the eggs and carefully score the surface several times so that the flavour of the spices can penetrate. Set aside.

3. Preheat a karahi (Balti pan) over a medium heat and add the oil. When hot, add the onion seeds followed by the onion, ginger, garlic and green chillies. Stir-fry for 6-7 minutes, until the onion slices begin to colour.

4. Add the ground coriander and cumin and stir-fry for 30 seconds, then add the warm water and aubergine. Bring to the boil, cover the karahi with a lid or piece of foil and cook over a medium heat for 5 minutes. The aubergines should sink now, so watch carefully to avoid overcooking. Add the gravy, prawns and eggs. Bring to the boil, cover the karahi again and reduce the heat to low. Cook for 3-4 minutes.

5. Add the garam masala and coriander leaves. Stir and cook for 1-2 minutes, then serve.

Preparation time: 20 minutes, plus cooking time for the Makhani Gravy
Cooking time: 20 minutes

Serve with Tala hua Chawal or Mewa Pulao (see page 104 or 106).

Suitable for freezing if frozen prawns are used.

Jhinga-Khumb-Kheema-Mattar

(Prawns with Mushrooms, Minced Lamb and Peas)
Serves 4-5

Fresh prawns will produce the best results in this recipe. However, as they are much more expensive, you can use peeled and cooked frozen prawns as long as you thaw and drain them first. It is also important to cook them only very briefly to retain the soft and juicy texture. You simply need to warm them through in the sauce.

45 ml (3 tbsp) sunflower, corn or vegetable oil
2.5 ml (½ tsp) cumin seeds
2.5 ml (½ tsp) crushed dried chillies
1 small onion, finely chopped
225 g (8 oz) minced lamb or beef
5 ml (1 tsp) Ginger Paste (see page 12)
5 ml (1 tsp) Garlic Paste (see page 12)
2.5 ml (½ tsp) ground anise (ajowain)
5 ml (1 tsp) ground coriander
2.5 ml (½ tsp) ground turmeric

2.5 ml (½ tsp) chilli powder
225 g (8 oz) closed cup mushrooms, sliced
450 ml (15 fl oz) Makhani Gravy (see page 13)
5 ml (1 tsp) salt, or to taste
2.5 ml (½ tsp) dried mint
*225 g (8 oz) shelled fresh prawns or cooked and peeled
   frozen prawns, thawed and drained*
100 g (4 oz) frozen garden peas
2.5 ml (½ tsp) Balti Garam Masala (see page 10)
45 ml (3 tbsp) chopped fresh coriander leaves

1. Preheat a karahi (Balti pan) over a medium heat and add the oil. When hot, but not smoking, add the cumin and crushed chillies, let them sizzle for 15 seconds and add the onion. Stir-fry for 3-4 minutes, until the onion is beginning to soften, but do not allow it to colour.
2. Add the mince and stir-fry for 2-3 minutes, then add the ginger, garlic, ground anise, coriander, turmeric and chilli powder. Stir-fry for 2-3 minutes and add 75 ml (3 fl oz) water. Continue to stir-fry for a further 2-3 minutes or until the water evaporates.
3. Add the mushrooms and stir-fry for 1 minute. Add 75 ml (3 fl oz) water and stir-fry until the mushrooms begin to look quite moist.
4. Stir in the gravy and stir until the contents begin to bubble. Reduce the heat to low and cook, uncovered, for 5 minutes, stirring once or twice.
5. Add the salt, mint, prawns and frozen peas. Stir until it begins to bubble again, then cook for 3-7 minutes depending on the type of prawns used. Add the garam masala and coriander leaves, then stir and cook for 1-2 minutes before serving.

Preparation time: 15 minutes, plus cooking time for the Makani Gravy
Cooking time: 25-35 minutes

Serve with any bread or plain boiled basmati rice and a raita.

Suitable for freezing if fresh prawns are used.

✥***Cook's tip:*** Use leftovers to make an instant pulao by mixing with Sada Pulao (see page 104). Serve with Kadhai Dhal Makhani (see page 85).

Murgh-Aloo-Chole

(Chicken with Potatoes and Chick Peas)
Serves 4-6

This is a super-quick dish which you can make even more quickly if you have any leftover Do-Piaza Murgh, Kadhai Murgh or Murgh-Jeera (see page 36, 42 or 48). Cook only the potatoes and chick peas, reducing all the spices to half the quantity given and mix with 175 g (6 oz) cooked chicken.

25 g (1 oz) ghee
5 ml (1 tsp) shahi jeera (royal cumin)
5 cm (2 inch) piece cassia bark or cinnamon stick, halved
1 fresh green chilli, seeded and chopped
5 ml (1 tsp) Ginger Paste (see page 12)
5 ml (1 tsp) Garlic Paste (see page 12)
5 ml (1 tsp) ground coriander
5 ml (1 tsp) ground cumin
300 g (10 oz) boned chicken thighs or breast, skinned and cut into 5 cm (2 inch) cubes

50 g (2 oz) natural yogurt
2.5 ml (½ tsp) chilli powder, or to taste
400 g (14 oz) can of chick peas, drained and rinsed
450 ml (15 fl oz) Makhani Gravy (see page 13)
150 ml (¼ pint) warm water
225 g (8 oz) pre-boiled potatoes, peeled and cut into 5 cm (2 inch) cubes
5 ml (1 tsp) salt, or to taste
2.5 ml (½ tsp) Balti Garam Masala (see page 10)
45 ml (3 tbsp) chopped fresh coriander leaves

1. Preheat a karahi (Balti pan) over a medium heat and add the ghee. When hot, but not smoking, add the shahi jeera, cassia or cinnamon and green chilli, let them sizzle for 15 seconds and add the ginger and garlic. Stir-fry for 30 seconds and add the ground coriander and cumin. Stir-fry for a further 30 seconds.
2. Stir in the chicken and yogurt and increase the heat to high. Stir-fry for 4-5 minutes and add the chilli powder. Stir-fry for a further 1-2 minutes.
3. Add the drained chick peas and stir-fry for 2-3 minutes, then add the gravy and warm water. Bring to the boil, reduce the heat to low, cover the karahi with a lid or piece of foil and cook for 15-20 minutes, stirring occasionally.
4. Add the cooked potatoes and salt, simmer uncovered for 4-5 minutes and add the garam masala and coriander leaves. Stir and cook for 1 minute, then serve.

Preparation time: 15-20 minutes, plus cooking time for the potatoes and Makhani Gravy
Cooking time: 35 minutes

Serve with any bread or Tala hua Chawal (see opposite) and a raita.

Suitable for freezing, but freeze at the end of step 3.
Thaw completely and proceed from step 4.

RICE AND BREAD

For the early settlers, wheat and barley were their staple diet. It was not until later that rice was discovered. Today we are lucky to have the wonderful and unique basmati rice which grows extensively in the foothills of the Himalayas. Basmati rice grown in Pakistan is also of exceptionally high quality. The North West Frontier, where Balti cuisine is most prevalent, has retained the original Balti tradition of eating bread rather than rice. While Pakistan-occupied Kashmir thrives on wheat, rice is the staple food in Indian Kashmir. Rice breaks the monotony of eating bread with every Balti meal and is in keeping with a traditional Indian meal which consists of both bread and rice. Included in this chapter are some delicious unleavened breads, which are traditionally cooked on an iron griddle, known as a 'tava'. A heavy-based frying pan is essential to cook these breads successfully. Naans are cooked in a tandoor, but the recipes here have been adapted for cooking in a domestic oven.

Tala hua Chawal

(Fried Rice)
Serves 4

The flavour of this rice is mild enough to blend with almost any meat, poultry and vegetable dish. It is quick and easy and a little more special than plain boiled rice.

225 g (8 oz) basmati rice, washed and soaked for 30 minutes
50 g (2 oz) ghee or unsalted butter
5 ml (1 tsp) shahi jeera (royal cumin)
6 green cardamom pods, the top of each pod split to release the flavour

5 cm (2 inch) piece cassia bark or cinnamon stick, halved
2.5 ml (½ tsp) salt, or to taste
15 ml (1 tbsp) broken cashew pieces (optional)
475 ml (16 fl oz) warm water

1. Drain the rice thoroughly and set aside. Melt the ghee or butter in a heavy-based, non-stick saucepan over a medium heat. When the fat is hot, add the shahi jeera, cardamom and cassia or cinnamon and stir-fry for 15-20 seconds.
2. Add the rice, salt and cashew nuts, if using. Stir-fry the rice for 3-4 minutes, then add the water. Bring to the boil and allow to boil steadily for 1 minute. Reduce the heat to low, cover the pan tightly and cook for 10-12 minutes.
3. Remove the pan from the heat and allow to stand for 10-15 minutes. Fork through the rice and serve.

Preparation time: 5 minutes, plus soaking and resting time
Cooking time: 12-15 minutes

Serve with almost any curry.

Suitable for freezing.

✦*Cook's tip:* Mix with any left-over meat, poultry or vegetable dish to create a quick and tasty pulao. Reheat the curry first and reduce the sauce to a paste-like consistency before mixing with the rice.

Golden Rules for Cooking Basmati Rice

← Put the rice in a bowl and wash and drain it two or three times. You will find that the water is quite milky in the beginning, but gets clearer and clearer by about the third wash. Soak the rice for 30 minutes, then drain thoroughly. This process removes most of the milling starch which would otherwise make the rice sticky when cooked.

← Once you have placed the lid on the saucepan and set the timer, do not be tempted to peep! Lifting the lid will result in the loss of the steam which is vital for successfully cooking rice, whether it is plain, pulao or fried .

← When the cooking is finished, do not stir the rice immediately. Freshly cooked rice is very fragile and should be allowed to stand for 10-15 minutes before serving. It will keep hot for up to 45 minutes, so you need not worry.

← Once the rice has had the required resting time, gently fork through it to separate the grains and serve.

Sada Pulao

(Plain Pilau Rice)
Serves 4

225 g (8 oz) basmati rice, washed and soaked for
 30 minutes
50 g (2 oz) ghee or unsalted butter
1 large onion, finely sliced
4 green cardamom pods, the top of each pod split to
 release the flavour
4 cloves

two 5 cm (2 inch) pieces cassia bark or cinnamon
 stick, halved
2.5 ml (½ tsp) ground turmeric
2.5 ml (½ tsp) salt
475 ml (16 fl oz) warm water
fresh coriander sprigs, to garnish

1. Drain the rice thoroughly and set aside. Melt the ghee or butter in a heavy-based, non-stick saucepan over a medium heat. When the fat is hot, add the onion and fry for 9-10 minutes, until the slices are well-browned. Remove them with a slotted spoon and drain on absorbent kitchen paper. Set aside.

2. In the fat remaining in the pan, sizzle the cardamom, cloves and cassia or cinnamon for 15-20 seconds. Add the drained rice, turmeric, salt and half the fried onion. Reduce the heat and stir-fry the rice for 1 minute, then add the water. Increase the heat to high and bring the water to the boil. Allow to boil steadily for 1 minute, then reduce the heat to low. Cover the pan tightly and cook for 10-12 minutes without lifting the saucepan lid.

3. Remove the pan from the heat and set aside, undisturbed, for 10-15 minutes. Fork through the rice and transfer to a serving dish. Garnish with the remaining fried onion slices and sprigs of fresh coriander and serve.

Preparation time: 10 minutes, plus soaking and resting time
Cooking time: 20 minutes

Suitable for freezing.

Biryani Khyberi

(Afghan Biryani)
Serves 4-6

The Pathans (original inhabitants of Afghanistan), were the creators of this superb dish. The recipe travelled with them through the Khyber Pass, the great gateway in the Hindu Kush range of mountains, through which many of the invaders entered India. Situated close to the North West Frontier, the Khyber pass is a long, narrow valley which links Kabul, in Afghanistan, to Peshawar in Pakistan. Don't be put off by the long list of ingredients. Once you have marinated the chicken, the method is quite straight-forward, the chicken and rice cook together, needing no attention at all.It is well worth the effort for dinner parties and special occasions.

5 ml (1 tsp) saffron strands
50 ml (2 fl oz) hot milk
700 g (1½ lb) boned chicken thighs or breast, cut into
    2.5 cm (1 inch) cubes
75 g (3 oz) natural yogurt
10 ml (2 tsp) Ginger paste (see page 12)
2 teaspoons Garlic paste (see page 12)
7.5 ml (1½ tsp) salt
75 g (3 oz) ghee
1 large onion, finely sliced
1-2 long, slim dried red chillies, chopped
10 ml (2 tsp) coriander seeds

5 ml (1 tsp) cumin seeds
2.5 ml (½ tsp) black peppercorns
2.5 cm (1 inch) piece cassia bark or cinnamon stick,
    broken up
seeds from 2 black cardamom pods
4 cloves
2 mace blades
15 ml (1 tbsp) raw cashew pieces
15 ml (1 tbsp) poppy seeds
350 g (12 oz) basmati rice, washed but not
    soaked

1. Pound the saffron with a pestle and mortar, then soak it in the hot milk. Set aside.
2. Put the chicken in a mixing bowl and add the yogurt, ginger, garlic, half the salt and half the saffron milk along with the saffron strands. Mix the ingredients thoroughly, cover the bowl and leave to marinate in the refrigerator for 2-4 hours, or overnight. Bring to room temperature before cooking.
3. Melt 50 g (2 oz) of the ghee in a large, heavy-based saucepan over a medium heat and fry the onions for 8-10 minutes, until they are lightly browned. In a coffee grinder, half grind the chillies, coriander seeds, cumin seeds, black peppercorns, cassia or cinnamon, cadamom seeds, cloves and mace. Add the cashew pieces and poppy seeds and grind until fine. Add this mixture to the onion and stir-fry for 1 minute, then add the chicken along with any marinade left in the bowl. Increase the heat to high and stir-fry for 1 minute, then reduce the heat to low for 4-5 minutes to enable the chicken to just heat through.
4. Meanwhile, bring 1.1 litre (2 pints) water to the boil and add the rice. Bring back to the boil and allow to boil steadily for 1 minute. Drain the rice and pile it on top of the chicken in the pan and spread it evenly.
5. Dissolve the remaining salt in 50 ml (2 fl oz) water and sprinkle it evenly on the rice. Melt the remaining ghee. Drizzle the remaining saffron milk and the melted ghee over the rice. Soak a clean tea towel in cold water and ring out – it should be wet, but not dripping. Cover the saucepan loosely with the wet towel in such a way that the cloth hangs slightly inside the saucepan, but does not touch the rice. Cover with a piece of foil, then place the lid securely on the foil and cloth, bring together all the corners of the tea towel and rest them on top of the lid. The pan is now completely sealed to enable the rice and the chicken to cook in the steam created inside. Reduce the heat to very low (use a diffuser, if necessary) and let the biryani cook for 1 hour. Traditionally, biryani is served in the cooking pot. However, it can be transferred to a serving dish, if wished.

Preparation time: 25-30 minutes, plus marinating time
Cooking time: 1¼ hours

Suitable for freezing. Thaw slowly in the refrigerator, then reheat.

Mewa Pulao

(Dry Fruit Pulao)
Serves 6

Kashmir produces a great variety of fruits and nuts and this fruity pulao is a speciality of the region. It is ideal for a dinner party or as a Sunday special. It can be cooked equally successfully in a karahi (Balti pan) or a saucepan.

2.5 ml (½ tsp) saffron strands
75 ml (3 fl oz) hot milk
50 g (2 oz) ghee or unsalted butter
6 green cardamom pods, the top of each pod split to release the flavour
4 cloves
5 ml (1 tsp) shahi jeera (royal cumin)
two 5 cm (2 inch) pieces cassia bark or cinnamon sticks, broken up

1 fresh green chilli, seeded and chopped
25 g (1 oz) blanched and slivered almonds
25 g (1 oz) walnut pieces
300 g (10 oz) basmati rice, washed and soaked for 30 minutes and drained
25 g (1 oz) dried, ready-to-eat apricots, sliced
25 g (1 oz) seedless raisins
5 ml (1 tsp) salt, or to taste
525 ml (18 fl oz) warm water

1. Pound the saffron with a pestle and mortar, then soak it in the hot milk. Set aside.
2. Heat the ghee or butter in a saucepan, karahi or wok and add the cardamom pods, cloves, shahi jeera, cassia or cinnamon and fresh chilli. Stir-fry for 15 seconds.
3. Add the almonds and walnuts and stir-fry for 30 seconds, then add the rice, apricots, raisins, salt and saffron milk, including the softened strands. Stir and mix thoroughly.
4. Pour in the warm water, bring to the boil and reduce the heat to low. Cover the pan and cook for 10-12 minutes without lifting the lid. Remove the pan from heat and set aside, undisturbed for 10-15 minutes. Fork through the pulao and transfer it to a serving dish.

Preparation time: 10 minutes, plus soaking and resting time
Cooking time: 12-14 minutes

Serve with Murgh Tikka Makhani (see page 48) or Makhani Murgh (see page 32), accompanied by a raita.

Suitable for freezing.

Mewa Pulao

Balti Naan

(Balti Bread)
Makes 3

'Naan', which came to India with the ancient Persians, is the Mid-eastern word for bread. Manufacturers of naan in Britain label their packaging 'naan bread', which means 'bread bread' ! The bread that is known as a 'Balti Naan' in Britain, is served as a 'Family Naan' in the Bukhara restaurants in India. A Balti or Family Naan differs from other naans only in its size; I have had one served to me and my family that was 50 cm (20 inches) long and 30 cm (12 inches) wide! The size of a Balti Naan greatly facilitates the communal eating habits: the bigger the naan, the easier it is for everyone to reach from all corners!

450 g (1 lb) plain flour
7.5 ml (1½ tsp) baking powder
5 ml (1 tsp) salt
5 ml (1 tsp) sugar

10 ml (2 tsp) onion seeds (kalonji)
50 g (2 oz) ghee or unsalted butter, melted
225 ml (8 fl oz) lukewarm milk
1 small egg, beaten

1. Put the flour, baking powder, salt, sugar and onion seeds in a large mixing bowl and mix well. Add the ghee or butter and work into the flour with your fingertips. Alternatively, put all these ingredients used so far in a food processor with a dough hook attachment and mix for a few seconds.

2. Gradually add the milk and mix until a soft dough is formed, then knead for 1-2 minutes. If mixing by hand, transfer the dough to a pastry board and knead for 3-4 minutes; the dough should now feel soft and smooth and not stick to your fingers. If using a food processor it should have stopped sticking to the sides of the bowl and hook. Place the dough in a warmed bowl and cover with a damp cloth or cling film. Allow to rest for 1-1½ hours.

3. Preheat the oven to 220°C (425°F) Mark 7. Line a large baking sheet with greased greaseproof paper or baking parchment and preheat it.

4. Lightly grease a large pastry board or a flat work surface and a rolling pin. Divide the dough into three equal-sized pieces and mould each one to a smooth round ball. Flatten each ball and roll out to a 20 cm (8 inch) disc. Gently pull the lower end to form a teardrop shape and roll it out again to make it about 40 cm (16 inches) long, maintaining the teardrop shape. The widest part should be about 23 cm (9 inches) and the narrowest 10 cm (4 inches).

5. If you find it difficult to make the teardrop shape, you can make the naans round or square. The traditional shape is due to the fact that the naan is hung on the wall of the tandoor, the Indian clay oven, and gravity causes the naan to stretch at the bottom, forming a teardrop shape.

6. Place one naan at a time on the prepared baking sheet and brush with the beaten egg. Bake in the top of the oven for 8-9 minutes. Wrap the cooked naan in a large piece of foil lined with absorbent kitchen paper to keep it warm while baking the other two.

Preparation time: 10-15 minutes, plus resting time
Cooking time: 25-30 minutes

Serve with any Balti meal.

Suitable for freezing.

Kheema Naan

(Naan with Spicy Mince Stuffing)
Makes 6

Kheema Naan makes a meal in itself; all you need is a range of delicious dips and raitas, add one or two types of kababs to the menu and you have a lovely informal meal to enjoy with friends. Kheema Naan is also delicious with vegetable curries.

500 g (1 lb 2 oz) self-raising flour
5 ml (1 tsp) salt
10 ml (2 tsp) sugar
1 sachet (6 g) easy blend dried yeast
75 g (3 oz) ghee or unsalted butter
225 ml (8 fl oz) soda water
50 g (2 oz) natural yogurt
For the filling:
450 g (1 lb) lean minced lamb
10 ml (2 tsp) Garlic Paste (see page 12)
10 ml (2 tsp) Ginger Paste (see page 12)

75 g (3 oz) onion, chopped
15 ml (1 tbsp) ground coriander
10 ml (2 tsp) ground cumin
5 ml (1 tsp) Balti Garam Masala (page 10)
1 fresh green chilli, seeded and chopped
30 ml (2 tbsp) chopped fresh mint leaves or 7.5 ml
　(1½ tsp) dried mint
15 g (½ oz) chopped fresh coriander leaves, including
　the tender stalks
2.5 ml (½ tsp) Tandoori Masala (page 11)
5 ml (1 tsp) salt, or to taste

1. In a large mixing bowl, mix together the flour, salt, sugar and dried yeast. Rub in the ghee or butter and gradually add the soda water. Mix until a soft dough is formed. Transfer the dough to a pastry board and knead for 4-5 minutes, or until it stops sticking to the board and your fingers. Alternatively, put the flour, salt, sugar, yeast and ghee or butter in a food processor and process for a few seconds. Add the soda water and knead until the dough stops sticking to the bowl and the dough hook.

2. As soon as the dough is ready, put it in a large plastic food bag and tie up the opening. Put the bag of dough in a bowl and leave it in a warm place, such as the airing cupboard or top of the boiler, for 1-1½ hours.

3. Meanwhile, put all the ingredients for the filling in the food processor and mix until the mixture turns to a fine paste. Divide into six portions and set aside.

4. When the dough is ready, remove it from the bag, knock back and divide into six equal portions. Cover and leave to prove for 15-20 minutes.

5. Meanwhile, preheat the oven to 220°C (425°F) Mark 7. Line a large baking sheet with greased greaseproof paper or non-stick baking parchment.

6. Take a portion of dough and flatten it by stretching and patting so that it is large enough to fully cover a portion of the minced lamb mixture. Place the mince in the centre and close it up by sealing the edges tightly, then flatten it gently to make a round cake. Dust it in a little dry flour, roll out to a 12.5 cm (5 inch) disc, then gently pull the lower end to make a tear-drop shape. If you find the tear-drop shape difficult to do, you can make them round.

7. Place two or three naan on the baking sheet and brush the surface of each with the yogurt. Bake in the upper part of the oven for 9-10 minutes.

Preparation time: 20-30 minutes, plus proving time
Cooking time: 20-30 minutes

Serve with any vegetable curry or dhal.

Suitable for freezing.

Sheermal

(Milk Bread)
Makes 8

The word 'sheer' means milk and Sheermal, a rich Muslim speciality, is traditionally made with equal quantities of milk and ghee. There are several versions, and this is my version which you can serve for special occasions or reserve it as as a treat.

450 g (1 lb) plain flour
5 ml (1 tsp) baking powder
5 ml (1 tsp) salt
15 ml (1 tbsp) sugar
175 g (6 oz) ghee or unsalted butter, melted
100 ml (4 fl oz) single cream

200 ml (7 fl oz) warm milk
5 ml (1 tsp) saffron strands, pounded
extra flour for dusting
15 ml (1 tbsp) shahi jeera (royal cumin)
a little melted butter for brushing (optional)

1. Put the flour, baking powder, salt and sugar in a large mixing bowl and mix well. Add half the melted ghee or butter and work it in with your fingertips. Work in the cream. Reserve 60 ml (4 tbsp) of the milk, gradually add the remainder to the flour and knead until a soft dough is formed. Alternatively, put all these ingredients in a food processor with a dough hook attachment and process until the dough is formed.

2. If you are mixing by hand, transfer the dough to a pastry board and add the remaining melted fat. Knead for 2-3 minutes, or until the dough is smooth, soft and it stops sticking to the board and your fingers. If mixing in the processor, add the remaining melted fat and knead for 1-2 minutes or until the dough is soft and the bowl and dough hook have no dough sticking to them.

3. Cover the dough with a damp cloth and set aside for 30 minutes. Meanwhile, preheat the oven to 220°C (425°F) Mark 7. Bring the reserved milk to the boil and add the saffron strands; stir well and set aside. Line a baking sheet with greased greaseproof paper or baking parchment.

4. Divide the dough in half and make four balls out of each half. Flatten each ball to a round cake, dust lightly in flour and roll out to a disc about 20 cm (8 inches) in diameter. Carefully lift it on to the baking sheet. Brush generously with saffron milk and sprinkle with a little shahi jeera. Bake in the top of the oven for 7-8 minutes. Line a piece of foil with absorbent kitchen paper and place the cooked Sheermal on one end. Brush with melted butter, if using, and fold the lined foil over it to keep the bread warm while cooking the remainder.

Preparation time: 15 minutes, plus resting time
Cooking time: 30-35 minutes

Serve with Rista, Zaffrani Murgh Musallam or Murgh-Saag (see pages 28, 40 or 41).

Suitable for freezing. Thaw and sprinkle water on both sides, then heat through in a preheated hot oven for 3-4 minutes.

Sheermal (left) and Pyaz-Pudina ki Roti (right)

Pyaz-Pudina ki Roti

(Onion and Mint-flavoured Bread)
Makes 8

This bread with its distinctive flavours of mint and onion is good enough to eat on its own! The atta (chapatti flour) gives it an enticing earthy flavour. Atta, which is sold in Indian shops, is the entire wheat kernel ground to a fine powder. You can use wholemeal flour, but the texture is much coarser and makes Indian breads rather brittle. An equal quantity of wholemeal flour and strong plain white flour will produce a better result.

450 g (1 lb) atta
5 ml (1 tsp) onion seeds (kalonji)
5 ml (1 tsp) salt
50 g (2 oz) ghee or unsalted butter, softened
30 ml (2 tbsp) finely chopped fresh mint leaves

1 onion, coarsely grated
100 ml (4 fl oz) warm water
extra flour for dusting
oil for shallow frying

1. To make the dough by hand, put the atta, onion seeds and salt into a large mixing bowl and mix well. Rub in the ghee or butter. Stir in the mint and onion and mix thoroughly. Add the water a little at a time, as the absorbency level of flour varies from brand to brand. Mix until a rough dough is formed, then transfer it to a pastry board and knead for 4-5 minutes, or until it stops sticking to the board and your fingers. Add a little more atta, if necessary.

2. To make the dough in a food processor with a dough hook attachment, put all the ingredients in the processor and knead until the dough feels smooth and soft and it does not stick to the bowl or dough hook.

3. Cover the dough with a damp cloth and set aside for 20-30 minutes.

4. Divide the dough in half and make four portions out of each half. Rotate each portion between your palms to make a smooth round ball and then flatten it to a cake.

5. Preheat a cast-iron griddle or a heavy-based frying pan over a medium-high heat. Dust each cake lightly in the extra flour and roll out to an 18 cm (7 inch) disc or roti. Keep the flattened cakes covered during the rolling out process.

6. Place the roti on the griddle and cook for about 1 minute, then turn it over. Spread about 15 ml (1 tbsp) oil on the cooked side and turn it over again. Cook for 45-50 seconds, or until brown spots appear. Check this by lifting the roti gently.

7. Spread another 15 ml (1 tbsp) oil on the second side and turn it over. Cook as for the first side, until brown spots appear.

8. Line a large piece of foil with absorbent kitchen paper and place the cooked roti on one end of the lined foil. Fold the other end over to keep it covered until all the rotis are cooked. Seal the edges to keep the rotis hot. They will keep hot for 30-40 minutes.

Preparation time: 15-20 minutes, plus resting time
Cooking time: 30-35 minutes

Serve with any lamb dish.

Suitable for freezing. Reheat from frozen under a preheated medium grill, about 12.5 cm (5 inches) below the element, for 2-3 minutes, until heated through, turning the bread over halfway through.

Masala Roti

(Spicy Bread)
Makes 12

The word 'masala' refers to a blend of spices and 'roti' is simply bread. Most Indian breads are made of whole-wheat flour known as atta, also known as chapatti flour, which is sold in Asian shops. If you cannot get atta, use wholemeal bread flour but you will need to sieve it to get the fine texture and, unfortunately, this will remove all the goodness of the bran and wheatgerm.

700 g (1½ lb) atta
5 ml (1 tsp) salt
7.5 ml (1½ tsp) shahi jeera (royal cumin)
5 ml (1 tsp) onion seeds (kalonji)
10 ml (2 tsp) ground cumin
2.5 ml (½ tsp) freshly ground black pepper

50 g (2 oz) ghee, butter or margarine
400 ml (13 fl oz) warm water
15 g (½ oz) finely chopped fresh coriander leaves
flour for dusting
ghee or oil for brushing

1. To make the dough by hand, put the atta, salt, shahi jeera, onion seeds, ground cumin and pepper into a large mixing bowl and mix well with your fingertips. Rub in the fat until well blended. Gradually add the water, a little at a time, as the absorbency level of flour varies greatly. When a rough, fairly moist dough is formed, transfer it to a pastry board and add the coriander leaves. Knead until the dough is soft, pliable and does not stick to your fingers or the board.
2. To make the dough in a food processor with a dough hook attachment, put the ingredients in the processor and knead until the dough feels smooth and soft and it does not stick to the bowl.
3. Cover the dough with a damp cloth or put into a plastic food bag and leave it to rest for 20-30 minutes.
4. Divide the dough into four equal parts and break off or cut three equal portions from each part. Flatten each portion by first rotating it between your palm and then pressing it down to a round cake. Cover them again with the cloth and preheat a cast-iron or other heavy griddle over a medium heat for 2-3 minutes.
5. Meanwhile, dust one of the cakes in flour and roll it out to an 18 cm (7 inch) disc. Ease the disc away from the board, place it on the griddle and cook for 1 minute. Turn it over and spread 5 ml (1 tsp) melted ghee or oil on the entire surface of the cooked side. Allow the underside to cook for 30-40 seconds. Turn the roti over and allow the oiled side to cook for 30-40 seconds. During this time spread oil or ghee on the second side as you have done for the first side. Lift the roti to check for brown patches on the underside. As soon as brown patches appear, turn it over. Cook the second oiled side until brown patches appear. Transfer to a plate lined with absorbent kitchen paper. Cook the rest of the rotis the same way.

Preparation time: 15-20 minutes, plus resting time
Cooking time: 20-25 minutes

Serve with Aloo Gosht, Kheema Do-Piaza or Kadhai Murgh (see pages 15, 29 or 42).

Suitable for freezing. Reheat from frozen on a preheated griddle until heated through.

✦***Cook's tip:*** These rotis are delicious with any kabab placed on them and topped with a chutney or raita. Roll the bread into a tube and serve.

CHUTNEYS AND RAITAS

Small side dishes of chutneys and raitas have always been a part and parcel of any traditional Indian meal – and Balti meals are no exception. A good store of relishes makes meals more interesting and exciting.

Pudina-Dhaniya ki Chutney

(Mint and Coriander Relish)

30 ml (2 tbsp) chopped fresh mint leaves
15 g (½ oz) chopped fresh coriander leaves including
  the tender stalks
1 fresh green chilli, seeded and chopped
1 small garlic clove, peeled and chopped
5 ml (1 tsp) Ginger Paste (see page 12)

2.5 ml (½ tsp) salt, or to taste
5 ml (1 tsp) sugar
30 ml (2 tbsp) lemon juice
125 g (4 oz) natural yogurt made with whole milk
25 g (1 oz) ground almonds

1. Put all the ingredients in a blender or food processor and process until smooth. Transfer to a serving dish and chill in the refrigerator for at least 2 hours to allow the different flavours to develop.

Badam aur Phalon ki Chutney

(Almond and Fruit Relish)
Makes about 400 g (14 oz)

50 g (2 oz) blanched almonds, roughly chopped
25 g (1 oz) sultanas
225 ml (8 fl oz) boiling water
1 pomegranate
25 g (1 oz) dried ready-to-eat apricots, chopped
5 ml (1 tsp) ground cumin

2.5 ml (½ tsp) ground coriander
2.5 ml (½ tsp) chilli powder
2.5 ml (½ tsp) salt or to taste
10 ml (2 tsp) caster sugar
30 ml (2 tbsp) lemon juice

1. Soak the almonds and sultanas in the boiling water for 30 minutes.
2. Cut the pomegranate in half and remove the seeds with a fork. Alternatively, it can be peeled like an orange. Discard the outer skin and remove the white pith and inner white membrane.
3. Put the almonds and sultanas, along with the water in which they were soaked, in a blender and add the remaining ingredients. Blend until smooth. Chill in the refrigerator before serving.

*Pudina-Dhaniya ki Chutney (top), Bandgobi aur Gajjar ka Raita (centre)
and Tamatar au Dhaniya ki Chutney (bottom)*

Seb ki Chutney

(Apple Chutney)
Serves 4-6

This delicious sweet 'n' sour chutney with its slightly hot flavour can be served as a side dish with kababs instead of raita. It will keep well in the refrigerator for several weeks.

15 ml (1 tbsp) sunflower or corn oil
2.5 ml (½ tsp) onion seeds (kalonji)
2.5 ml (½ tsp) cumin seeds
575 g (1¼ lb) cooking apples, peeled, cored and finely chopped
5 ml (1 tsp) Ginger Paste (see page 12)

5 ml (1 tsp) Garlic Paste (see page 12)
10 ml (2 tsp) ground cumin
2.5-5 ml (½-1 tsp) chilli powder
6 g (1¼ tsp) salt
75 g (3 oz) granulated sugar
25 g (1 oz) seedless raisins

1. Preheat a karahi (Balti pan) for 1-2 minutes and add the oil. When hot, but not smoking, add the onion seeds and cumin seeds followed by the apples, ginger, garlic, cumin and chilli powder. Stir-fry for 2-3 minutes.
2. Add the salt and sugar and stir-fry for 30 seconds. Reduce the heat to low, cover the pan with a lid or piece of foil and cook for 5 minutes.
3. Remove the lid, add the raisins and stir-fry for 4-5 minutes, or until the mixture has thickened. Remove from heat and allow to cool thoroughly. Transfer to a dry jar and store in the refrigerator.

Tamatar aur Dhaniya ki Chutney

(Tomato and Coriander Chutney)
Serves 4-6

This lovely chutney is enriched with ground almonds and uses canned tomatoes for their brilliant red colour. Combined with the fresh green of coriander, the dish has a striking appearance. Fresh Italian plum tomatoes can be used instead of canned ones, if preferred. The fresh green chillies used here are the long, slim variety generally used in Indian cooking. You can buy these from Indian shops or good greengrocers. If using Mexican chillies such as Jalapeno or Serrano, which are rather fleshy and pungent, use only half a chilli.

225 g (8 oz) chopped canned tomatoes, drained, or fresh tomatoes, skinned and chopped
15 g (½ oz) chopped fresh coriander leaves, including the tender stalks
25 g (1 oz) ground almonds
2.5 ml (½ tsp) salt, or to taste

1-2 fresh green chillies, seeded and chopped
1 garlic clove, peeled
3 spring onions, the white part only, chopped
10 ml (2 tsp) lemon juice
2.5 ml (½ tsp) sugar

1. Put all the ingredients in a blender and blend until smooth. Transfer to a serving dish, cover and chill in the refrigerator for 1-2 hours. It will keep for 5-6 days in the refrigerator.

Preparation time: 10 minutes, plus chilling time

Serve with any kababs, accompanied by fried or grilled pappodums.

Suitable for freezing.

Baigan Raita

(Aubergine Raita)
Serves 4-6

1 medium or 2 small aubergines, about 300 g (10 oz)
2 small garlic cloves, peeled and roughly chopped
12 mm (½ inch) piece fresh root ginger, peeled and roughly chopped
1 fresh green chilli, seeded and chopped

15 g (½ oz) fresh coriander leaves, including the tender stalks
50 g (2 oz) plain cottage cheese
50 g (2 oz) thick set whole milk natural yogurt
2.5 ml (½ tsp) salt, or to taste

1. Wash the aubergine and make two slits lengthways without cutting right through it. Preheat the grill to medium. Place the aubergine in the grill pan and cook under the grill, about 15 cm (6 inches) away from the element, for 12-15 minutes, turning it over frequently. Allow to cool, then cut in half lengthways. Scoop out the flesh and discard the skin. Purée the flesh and remaining ingredients until smooth. Chill before serving.

Bandgobi aur Gajjar ka Raita

(Cabbage and Carrot Raita)
Serves 4-6

100 g (4 oz) white cabbage, finely grated or chopped
100 g (4 oz) carrots, grated
75 g (3 oz) onion (preferably red), finely chopped
1 fresh green chilli, seeded and finely chopped
30 ml (2 tbsp) finely chopped coriander leaves

150 g (5 oz) thick set natural yogurt
10 ml (2 tsp) bottled mint sauce
5 ml (1 tsp) sugar
2.5 ml (½ tsp) salt, or to taste
25 g (1 oz) roasted, salted peanuts, lightly crushed

1. In a bowl, combine the first five ingredients. Beat the yogurt with a fork until smooth. Mix in the mint sauce and sugar, then add to the cabbage mixture. Cover and chill. Stir in the salt and peanuts just before serving.

Gobi Raita

(Cauliflower with Yogurt Dressing)
Serves 4

15 ml (1 tbsp) sunflower, corn or vegetable oil
2.5 ml (½ tsp) black mustard seeds
2.5 ml (½ tsp) cumin seeds
5 ml (1 tsp) Garlic Paste (see page 12)
1.25 ml (¼ tsp) crushed dried chillies

100 g (4 oz) cauliflower florets, divided into 1 cm (¾ inch) diameter pieces
2.5 ml (½ tsp) salt, or to taste
175 g (6 oz) thick set natural yogurt
2.5 ml (½ tsp) sugar

1. Preheat a karahi (Balti pan) over a medium heat for 2-3 seconds. Add the oil. When hot, but not smoking, add the mustard seeds. As soon as they pop, add the cumin and fry for 15 seconds. Add the garlic and chillies and fry for 30 seconds, or until the garlic begins to brown. Add the cauliflower and salt. Stir and mix, reduce the heat to low, then cover the karahi and sweat the cauliflower for 4-5 minutes. Allow to cool. Beat the yogurt and sugar together, then stir in the cauliflower, scraping in all the spices from the karahi.

DRINKS AND DESSERTS

As with traditional Indian meals, pure chilled water is the natural choice of drink to accompany a Balti meal. Early civilisations recognised the importance of purifying drinking water. This they did by using a unique method of filtering it through the lotus flower. Gradually, refreshing beverages were developed using fruits such as mangoes, grapes and bananas. Yogurt and buttermilk were also used to make healthy and nourishing drinks. During the cold months, winter spices such as cinnamon, cloves and cardamom were added to tea. These ingredients are known to create body heat; a natural and inexpensive way to keep warm in the bitter climate. Desserts are mainly made of fruits – cherries, apricots and plums – and dairy products.

Elaichi Coffee

(Cardamom Coffee)
Serves 4

Indian food and drink have always been associated with enticing flavours. Tea and coffee are no exceptions; there are times when we like to have a cup of aromatic coffee flavoured with spices.

6 green cardamom pods, the top of each pod split to release the flavour

200 ml (7 fl oz) milk
instant coffee and sugar to taste

1. Put the cardamom pods in a saucepan with 600 ml (1 pint) water and bring to the boil. Reduce the heat to low, cover and simmer for 5-6 minutes. Add the milk and bring to the boil again. Remove the pods and discard them. Put coffee and sugar in individual cups and pour the milky mixture over them. Stir and serve.

Jal Jeera

(Cumin-flavoured Drink)
Serves 6

15 ml (1 tbsp) cumin seeds
5 ml (1 tsp) black peppercorns
7.5 ml (1½ tsp) tamarind concentrate

18-20 fresh mint leaves
6 g (1¼ tsp) salt, or to taste

1. Preheat an iron griddle or heavy-based pan over a medium heat. Dry roast the cumin until the seeds release their aroma – this will only take about a minute. Remove from the hot griddle and allow to cool, then crush them with a rolling pin or a spoon. Put the peppercorns in a small plastic bag and crush them coarsely.
2. Put the cumin and peppercorns in a saucepan with the remaining ingredients and 1 litre (1¾ pints) water. Bring to the boil, then reduce the heat and simmer for 5 minutes. Cool slightly, then strain through a fine sieve or muslin. Serve hot or cold as an appetiser.

Jal Jeera (left) and Aam ki Mithi Lassi (right)

Aam ki Meethi Lassi

(Mango-flavoured Sweet Yogurt Drink)
Makes 1.2 litres (2 pints)

300 ml (½ pint) canned mango purée
75 g (3 oz) caster sugar

450 g (1 lb) whole milk natural yogurt
45 ml (3 tbsp) rose water

1. Put all the ingredients in a blender with 600 ml (1 pint) water and blend together. Pour into a jug and chill in the refrigerator for 2-3 hours.
2. Serve in tall glasses with crushed ice as a refreshing and nourishing drink at any time, or in wine glasses with meals.

Variation: Omit the mango purée and reduce the rose water to 30 ml (2 tbsp). To make a savoury lassi, omit the mango and reduce the sugar to about 10 ml (2 tsp). Add 7.5 ml (1½ tsp) salt, 10-12 fresh mint leaves and freshly ground black pepper to taste. Blend all the ingredients in a blender and chill.

Annanas ka Mitha

(Pineapple Dessert)
Serves 4

1 large ripe pineapple
5 cm (2 inch) piece cassia bark or cinnamon stick,
*   halved*
150 g (5 oz) granulated sugar
2.5 ml (½ tsp) saffron strands, pounded

50 g (2oz) seedless raisins
10 ml (2 tsp) ground arrowroot
15 g (½ oz) unsalted shelled pistachio nuts, lightly
*   crushed*

1. To peel and cut the pineapple, slice off the two ends and then cut the pineapple lengthways, into eight boat-shaped pieces. Next, remove the hard core from the centre of each piece. Remove the skin by peeling it from one end to the other with a sharp knife, using a sawing action. Make sure all the eyes are removed, then cut each piece into 5 cm (2 inch) pieces.
2. Bring 600 ml (1 pint) water to the boil in a karahi (Balti pan) or saucepan and add the pineapple and cassia or cinnamon. Bring back to the boil, cover the karahi with a lid or piece of foil and cook over medium heat for 12-15 minutes, until the pineapple is soft, but not mushy. Remove the pineapple with a slotted spoon and set aside. Discard the cassia or cinnamon.
3. Add the sugar to the cooking water and let it boil for 8-10 minutes, then add the pounded saffron, raisins and cooked pineapple. Cook for 4-5 minutes.
4. Blend the arrowroot with a little cold water and stir this into the bubbling sugar syrup. Stir and cook for 1 minute. Transfer to a serving dish and allow to cool completely, then chill in the refrigerator. Serve chilled, scattered with the pistachio nuts.

Variation: Use firm unripe pears or dessert apples instead of pineapple. Adjust the quantity of sugar to suit your taste.

Preparation time: 10-15 minutes, plus chilling time
Cooking time: 25-30 minutes

Paneer ka Mitha

(Indian Cheese Pudding)
Serves 4-6

Paneer, which is an excellent source of protein and minerals, has been used to make sweetmeats and desserts in India since ancient times.

25 g (1 oz) ghee or unsalted butter
25 g (1 oz) flaked almonds
25 g (1 oz) chopped walnut
2.5 ml (½ tsp) ground cardamom
2.5 ml (½ tsp) ground cinnamon
1.25 ml (¼ tsp) saffron strands, pounded

225 g (8 oz) Paneer (see page 13), coarsely grated
600 ml (1 pint) evaporated milk
100 g (4 oz) granulated sugar, or to taste
15 ml (1 tbsp) ground arrowroot
100 ml (4 fl oz) single cream
30 ml (2 tbsp) rose water

1. In a heavy-based saucepan, heat the ghee over a low heat. Add the almonds and walnuts and stir-fry for 1 minute, or until they are lightly browned. Remove half the nuts and set them aside.

2. Add the ground cardamom and cinnamon to the pan and stir fry for 15 seconds, then add the saffron, paneer, evaporated milk and sugar. Increase the heat and bring the milk to the boil, stirring frequently to ensure that it does not stick to the bottom of the pan. Reduce the heat to low and simmer for 5-6 minutes, stirring frequently.

3. In a small bowl, blend the arrowroot with a little water and stir into the milk. Cook for 2-3 minutes, stirring constantly. Remove from the heat and allow to cool for 10-15 minutes, then stir in the cream and rose water. Transfer to a serving dish and decorate with the reserved nuts. Serve warm or at room temperature.

Preparation time: 10 minutes
Cooking time: 12-15 minutes

Badam ki Kulfi

(Almond-flavoured Iced Dessert)
Serves 6-8

Kulfi is the most popular iced dessert in India. It is sometimes referred to as Indian ice cream, though it has a much denser texture. Traditionally, kulfi is frozen in cone-shaped metal moulds from which it's name is also derived. As far as its origin goes, it is believed that the Moguls imported kulfi from Kabul, although there is some evidence that it could have originated in India after the arrival of the Moguls. Kulfi moulds are available from Asian shops, or you can freeze the dessert in small jelly moulds or other small plastic moulds and containers. Ice lolly moulds are also suitable. The traditional containers are small, holding a generous 30 ml (2 tbsp) of the mixture – use this as a guide when choosing your container. Freezing in large ice cream containers is not suitable as you will have a very long wait for the kulfi to soften enough to cut it into pieces. It cannot be spooned or scooped like ice cream as it is fairly hard. The traditional way to make kulfi is to boil a large quantity of milk until it is reduced to half its original volume. A quicker way is to use evaporated milk. To serve, purée fresh mangoes when in season, drain and purée canned mangoes, or use ready-made mango purée, available in Asian shops.

600 ml (1 pint) evaporated milk
300 ml (½ pint) single cream
150 g (5 oz) granulated sugar
25 g (1 oz) ground almonds

2.5 ml (½ tsp) almond essence
To serve:
mango purée and shelled unsalted pistachio
    nuts, lightly crushed

1. Put all the ingredients, except the almond essence, in a heavy based saucepan and bring to the boil over a medium heat, stirring frequently to make sure that the milk does not stick to the bottom of the pan.
2. Reduce the heat to low and simmer for 5-6 minutes, stirring constantly. Remove from the heat and allow to cool completely. While the mixture is cooling, stir frequently to prevent a skin forming. When cooled, stir in the almond essence.
3. Fill your chosen containers with the mixture and freeze for 4-6 hours.
4. Leave the kulfi at room temperature for 5-6 minutes before removing it from the mould. If it is difficult to unmould, dip it in hot water for 15-20 seconds. Turn out on to individual plates. Traditionally, kulfi is placed horizontally on the plate and sliced so that it is easy to pick up with a spoon.
5. Surround the kulfi with mango purée and sprinkle the pistachio nuts on top.

Variation: During the summer months, serve kulfi with puréed strawberries or raspberries.

Preparation time: 5 minutes
Cooking time: 12-15 minutes

Annanas ka Mitha (top) and Badam ki Kulfi (bottom)

Malai Kheer Kesari

(Creamed Saffron Rice)
Serves 4-6

This popular dessert from Northern India combines the enticing aroma of basmati rice and rose water. Rose water is available from Indian and Pakistani grocers; it is made from the essence extracted from the petals of roses specially cultivated for culinary purposes.

600 ml (1 pint) fresh milk

2.5 ml (½ tsp) saffron strands, pounded

25 g (1 oz) ghee

50 g (2 oz) basmati rice, washed and soaked in cold
   water for 30 minutes and drained

25 g (1 oz) raw unsalted cashews, split

25 g (1 oz) seedless raisins

300 ml (½ pint) evaporated milk

50 g (2 oz) caster sugar

5 ml (1 tsp) ground cardamom

50 ml (2 fl oz) single cream

15 ml (1 tbsp) rose water

25 g (1 oz) dried ready-to-eat-apricots, sliced

15 g (½ oz) toasted flaked almonds

1. Put the fresh milk in a heavy-based saucepan and bring to the boil, stirring frequently to ensure that it does not stick to the bottom of the pan. Remove from the heat and set aside.

2. Put the saffron in a small bowl and add 30 ml (2 tbsp) of the hot milk. Set aside.

3. Preheat a karahi (Balti pan) or saucepan over a low heat and add the ghee. When the ghee has melted, add the rice, cashews and raisins and stir-fry for 2-3 minutes.

4. Add the hot milk, bring to the boil again, then reduce the heat to low and cook, uncovered, for 15 minutes, stirring occasionally. Add the evaporated milk, saffron milk and sugar, bring back to the boil, reduce the heat to low and cook for a further 15 minutes. Watch it carefully as it will thicken quite quickly at this point, and stir very frequently to prevent it sticking to the bottom of the pan.

5. Add the ground cardamom and cream. Cook for 1 minute, then remove from the heat and stir in the rose water. Serve hot or cold, decorated with the dried apricots and toasted almonds.

Preparation time: 10 minutes
Cooking time: 35-40 minutes

Shahi Sevian

(Rich Vermicelli Pudding)
Serves 6

This luxurious Muslim festive dish has all the characteristic features of Mogul cuisine. The Moguls came to India through the Khyber Pass and established the famous Mogul Dynasty with Delhi as its centre. The use of rose essence or rose water to flavour, and fresh rose petals to garnish the food are traditions practised by the royal chefs and followed even today by connoisseurs of Mogul food.

50 g (2 oz) ghee or unsalted butter
25 g (1 oz) shelled walnuts, chopped
25 g (1 oz) shelled, unsalted pistachio nuts
25 g (1 oz) seedless raisins
100 g (4 oz) plain vermicelli, broken up into small
* pieces*
2.5 ml (½ tsp) ground cardamom

2.5 ml (½ tsp) ground cinnamon
1.25 ml (¼ tsp) saffron strands, pounded
75 g (3 oz) caster sugar
300 ml (½ pint) single cream
45 ml (3 tbsp) rose water
handful of fresh rose petals (optional)

1. In a heavy-based saucepan, melt the ghee or butter over a medium heat and sauté the walnuts and pistachio nuts until they are lightly browned. Remove them with a slotted spoon and set aside.
2. In the fat remaining in the pan, stir-fry the raisins gently until they puff up, then remove them with a slotted spoon and set aside.
3. Add the the vermicelli to the fat and stir-fry for 4-5 minutes, or until the vermicelli is a rich brown colour. Sprinkle with the ground cardamom, cinnamon and saffron and stir-fry for 30 seconds.
4. Add the sugar and 300 ml (½ pint) water and stir until the sugar has dissolved. Stir in half the fried nuts and raisins. Cover the saucepan, reduce the heat to low and cook for 4-5 minutes, or until the vermicelli has absorbed all the water. Remove the pan from the heat.
5. Mix together the cream and rose water and pour it over the cooked vermicelli. Stir gently to mix, then transfer the vermicelli to a serving dish. Serve hot or at room temperature, decorated with the reserved fried nuts and raisins, and fresh rose petals, if using.

Preparation time: 5-10 minutes
Cooking time: 12-15 minutes

Sooji ka Halwa

(Soft Semolina Fudge)
Serves 4-5

Wheat and milk are the basis of the majority of Indian and Pakistani sweets. These are enriched with ghee, fruit and nuts, and some are delicately spiced. There are several types of halwas, all of which are fairly rich with a high fat content. This is my cousin's traditional recipe, but you can reduce the ghee or butter if you want to.

75 g (3 oz) raw unsalted, broken cashew pieces
175 g (6 oz) ghee or unsalted butter
175 g (6 oz) semolina

50 g (2 oz) seedless raisins
400 g (14 oz) can of sweetened condensed milk

1. In a coffee grinder, grind the cashews until fine. Set aside.
2. Grease a 20 cm (8 inch) plate lightly and set aside.
3. In a heavy-based saucepan, heat the ghee or butter over a medium heat. Add the semolina and stir-fry for 3-4 minutes. Reduce the heat slightly and add the raisins. Continue to stir-fry for 2-3 minutes, until the semolina is a rich golden colour.
4. Reduce the heat to low and add the ground cashews and the condensed milk. Cook, stirring constantly, until the semolina reaches a soft dough consistency and does not stick to the sides or bottom of the saucepan. This will take 3-4 minutes.
5. Remove from the heat and transfer the semolina to the greased plate. Spread it to cover the entire surface of the plate. Using a plastic scraper or a metal spoon, shape it into a large square. You can do this by pushing all the four sides inwards and levelling off any uneven parts so that you end up with a 15 cm (6 inch) square which will be about 2.5 cm (1 inch) thick. Allow to cool completely, then cut into squares or diamonds. It will stick to the knife and the base of the plate if you cut it too soon. Alternatively, the mixture can be set in a decorative mould and turned out while still warm. Allow to cool before serving.

Preparation time: 5 minutes
Cooking time: 10 minutes

Serve with Elaichi Coffee (see page 118) after a meal, or
any other time with tea or coffee.

INDEX

STOCKISTS AND SUPPLIERS OF INDIAN INGREDIENTS

London

Ali Cash and Carry
301-303 High Street
North
Manor Park
London E12 6SL

Asian Food Centre
544 Harrow Road
Maida Vale
London W9 3GG

Dadu's Limited
190-198 Upper Tooting
Road
London SW17 7EW

Housewife's C & C
14 Craven Park Road
Harlesden
London NW10 4AB

M & S Patel
380 Romford Road
Forest Gate
London E7 8BS

Noon foods C & C
183 Shepherds Bush
Market
Shepherds Bush
London
W12 8DF

Pak Cash and Carry
Ltd.
27 Stroud Green Road
Finsbury Park
London N4 3EF

Spice Shop and Off
Licence
115-117 Drummond
Street
Euston
London NW1 2HL

S. R. Butcher and
Grocer
27-29 West Green Road
Tottenham London
NW15 5BX

Sunrise Cash and Carry
355-357 High Road
Leyton
London E10 5NA

S.W. Foodstore
34-36 Electric Avenue
Brixton
London SW9

T. A. Cash and Carry
61 Hanbury Street
Aldgate
London E1 5JP

Berkshire

Medina Stores
27 Debeauvoir Road
Reading
Berkshire RG1 5NR

Edinburgh

Nastiuks
155-159 Bruntsfield
Place
Edinburgh
EH8 9AY

Essex

Shah Brothers
1 The Triangle
Langdon Hill
Basildon
Essex
SG16 6HF

Glasgow

Oriental Food Stores
303-305 Great Western
Road
Glasgow
G4 9HS

Humberside

Indian and Continental
Food Stores
69 Prince's Avenue
Hull
HU5 3QN

Kent

OK Cash and Carry
253 Canterbury Street
Gillingham
Kent ME7 5XE

Midddlesex

Asian Food Centre
175-177 Staines Road
Hounslow
Middlesex TW3 3LF

Trishul Cash and Carry
152-154 Pinner Road
Harrow
Middlesex HA1 4JJ

Surrey

Atif's Cash and Carry
Walton Road
Woking
Surrey

Spicyfoods C & C
460-462 London Road
Croydon
Surrey CRO 2SS

Yorkshire

Bhullar Brothers Ltd
44 Springwood Street
Huddersfield
West Yorkshire
HD1 4BE

All Indian ingredients can also be obtained by mail order from:

Natco Spices
T. Choithram and Sons
(Stores) Ltd
Lancelot Road
Wembley
Middx. HAO 2BG
Telephone: 0181 903
8311
Fax: 0181 900 1426